Blessed M. Tamayo

The New is Your Exit from the Old

Breaking to Breakthrough
The New is Your Exit from the Old
ISBN-978-0-578-62099-2

Copyright © 2020 -Blessed M.Tamayo
All rights reserved.
Printed in USA

No part of this publication may be reproduced or transmitted in any form or by any means, electronic or mechanical, including photocopying, or by any information storage and retrieval system, without permission in writing from the author/publisher. Request for permission to make copies of any part of the work should be sent to Blessed Tamayo at alaskasamatayo@hotmail.com or call (713-822-9362).

Cover art design by Blessed Tamayo

Scriptures marked NKJV are taken from the NEW KING JAMES VERSION (NKJV): Scripture taken from the NEW KING JAMES VERSION®. Copyright© 1982 by Thomas Nelson, Inc. Used by permission. All rights reserved.

Scriptures marked AMP are taken from the AMPLIFIED BIBLE (AMP): Scripture taken from the AMPLIFIED® BIBLE, Copyright © 1954, 1958, 1962, 1964, 1965, 1987 by the Lockman Foundation Used by Permission. (www.Lockman.org)

Scriptures marked NLT are taken from the HOLY BIBLE, NEW LIVING TRANSLATION (NLT): Scriptures taken from the HOLY BIBLE, NEW LIVING TRANSLATION, Copyright© 1996, 2004, 2007 by Tyndale House Foundation. Used by permission of Tyndale House Publishers, Inc., Carol Stream, Illinois 60188. All rights reserved. Used by permission.

All Scripture quotations are taken from THE MESSAGE, copyright © 1993, 1994, 1995, 1996, 2000, 2001, 2002 by Eugene H. Peterson. Used by permission of NavPress. All rights reserved. Represented by Tyndale House Publishers, Inc.

Scriptures marked CEV are taken from the CONTEMPORARY ENGLISH VERSION (CEV): Scripture taken from the CONTEMPORARY ENGLISH VERSION copyright© 1995 by the American Bible Society. Used by permission.

Table of Contents

ACKNOWLEDGEMENT	xi
ABOUT THE AUTHOR	xiii
FOREWORD	xv
OVERVIEW: Breaking Your Way to Breakthrough **-The Only Way to Break is Through**	**17**
What Does God Got Ourselves Into?	17
Vision: Conviction for our Mission Completion	*17*
Heaven Collides with Earth through Revelation	*19*
Above All Things	20
Our Earthly Spiritual Breakthrough	*22*
God's Realm Converging into our Natural World	*23*
Embracing God's Process of Breakthrough	24
The Divine Destiny of our Soul	26
The Three Manifesting as One	27
The Core Intention of this Book	28
Chapter One: Launching Pad for Breakthrough **-Breakthrough is a collaboration of God and man**	**29**
Launching Pad of the Supernatural	29
Chapter Two: The Pathway to Breakthrough **-What breaks self-dependency is God's supremacy**	**33**
Brokenness: A New Covenant Principle	33
The Controversy	*33*
What Brokenness is NOT	*35*

What Brokenness IS	36
Our Entry is Our Exit	37
Breaking Out from our Own Isaacs	39
'Nothing' Can but 'Some-One' Could	41
Breaking through our Gethsemane	43
Resonating our Being in Christ	47
Exaltation Precedes Submission and Humility	49

Chapter Three: Breaking unto Greatness
-Greatness breaks through from the inside out — **51**

We Break Through from the Inside Out	51
The Massive Potential of Small Beginnings	53
Greatness Goes Beyond Self	57
The Paradox of Greatness	59

Chapter Four: Breakthrough is Decisive
-Crossing over unto the magnitude of your destiny — **65**

Breakthrough Impacts Your World	65
Mediocrity: The Enemy of Breakthrough	67
Mediocrity Defined	67
What Causes Mediocrity?	68
Mediocrity Stinks	69
Mediocrity Blinds	70
Mediocrity Procrastinates	71
Mediocrity Compromises	72
Mediocrity is a Choice	73

Table of Contents

Breakthrough is Significant	74
Counter Steer Your Way to Breakthrough	75
Breakthrough Does Not Step on the Brake	76
Breakthrough is Record Breaking	77
Chapter Five: The Making of a Breakthrough **-Breakthrough happens in life's in-between**	**81**
God's Mercy: The Basis of Life's Continuity	81
What Happened in Between?	82
'Don't Take Them Out of this World'	*83*
'Sanctify Them in Your Truth'	*86*
God Defines a Man	88
Earthly Relevance of Heaven's Reality	90
Co-Laboring with God	*91*
Spiritual Encounter Spills over the Glory of God	*92*
We Become Moldable	92
The Proving of Our Will	95
An Established Footing	96
Life is Being, it is not Trying	*97*
Being Built Upon the Rock	*99*
Bridging the Gap	101
The Highlight of Shifting	103
Jesus - Our Point of Reference	105
Walk Ye in Him	*107*
The Keys of the Kingdom	107

Chapter Six: Hard-Wired for Breakthrough
-Breaking through is our default settings — **111**

Naturally Hard-Wired for Growth — 111

Believer's DNA – "Divine Nature Attributes" — 112

Walking on God's Preconfigured Good Works — 115

What Drives Our Perspective? — 122

From the Outside In — *124*

Boomeranging — 125

Simon Syndrome — 126

Get Away Drivers — 127

Rationing Excuses — *127*

Overdose of Exaggeration — 128

From the Inside Out — *130*

Revelation — 132

The Intriguing Question — *135*

Revelation has an Eternal Consequence — *138*

Conviction — 138

Wisdom — 140

Wisdom is in the Right Place at the Right Time — *140*

Compassion — 144

Blessing — 145

Anointing — 146

Flowing in the Measured Anointing — *147*

The Meek will Rule the Earth — *148*

Contingent to the Holy Spirit's Will	*149*
The Presence of God	150
It is an Inside Job	155
Revelation and Manifestation	156
Balance is the Way of Life	157
Growth Takes Care of Balance	*158*
Grandeur of Irrelevant Motion	*159*
Get'r Done is Better Than Later Done	*160*
Spirit, and Soul, and Body	*163*
Vital Versus Trivial	*164*
The Balance View of Grace	*166*
Man and God's Plan	170
Completing the Man of His Plan	*171*
Salvation, Righteousness, and Faith	173
Faith: An Insight to our Righteousness in Christ	*174*
We Reign When He Lord Over Us	175
Chapter Seven: Breaking through the Obvious -We realized His promise when we see as God sees	**177**
Positioning Yourself to See	177
Growth is Secured Where God Planted Us	*179*
Let Go of your Stick	*180*
Breaching the External	181
Trigger the Tigger	*185*
Breaking Out from our External Religiosity	186

Chapter Eight: Breakthrough Transcends Time
-Breakthrough affects your past, future, and present   **191**

The Divine Commodity of Time   191

The Immateriality of the Past   193

    Still Polishing the Chain of Your Past?   *195*

    Your Past has No Future   *196*

    Double Trouble   *197*

    The Old Cannot Handle the New   *198*

    What Deals the Old is the New   *199*

Living with the Anxiety of the Future   201

Living Where Reality is Taking Place   203

    Faith – A Present Spiritual Lifestyle to Live By   *203*

Chapter Nine: The Catalyst for Breakthrough
-God's grace shaped our past and forged our future   **207**

Forgiveness: Our God-given Restart Button   207

    The Means to Get Us Going   *208*

    Forgiveness is a Form of Giving of Self   *208*

Check the Roots   210

Chapter Ten: Keep on Breaking It Through
-The other side is awaiting our breakthrough   **217**

Launching Out into the Deep   217

Complication: The Great Divide   220

Running the Race of Faith   221

    Propelling   *222*

    Pressing In   *223*

Table of Contents

Breaking Out	*224*
Transitioning from Interruptions	224
Living in an Imperfect World with our Perfect God	*225*
Becoming Dissatisfiedly Satisfied	*226*
Seizing Our Moments with God	227
You Manifest What You Behold	232
Learning from Simon Peter	233
Breaking Forth into Joy	236
In Case You Fell in Between the Cracks	237
From Breakthrough to Breakthrough	239
Endnotes	**243**

ACKNOWLEDGEMENT

I would like to recognize God our Father who arranged my days on earth and determined my steps. I also want to acknowledge the Lord Jesus Christ who shared His life with us through His cross and resurrection. Furthermore, I am grateful of the Holy Spirit's constant revelation of the glory of Christ.

I salute my wife Josie and my two sons - Joshua and Ezekiel who constantly gives me their vote of confidence to pursue my calling in the Lord.

This book is also a token of my gratitude towards my mother, Maria Luisa Tamayo. She inspired me with her wisdom and perseverance.

I am thankful to Owen and Ruth Baker, missionaries to the Philippines from Tulsa, Oklahoma; they are my spiritual parents. Sitting under Papa Baker's teaching ministry imparted us the sensitivity of how to flow in the spirit of revelation. I cherished the moments on how he opened to us the scriptures, line upon line, precepts upon precepts, and here a little and there a little. In the process, we learned how to read and meditate on the Word. Though they no longer with us physically and they are enjoying the presence of Almighty in glory, I am grateful for sharing their spirit to us.

I am also grateful to Dick and Kay Leslie, who taught me the value of relationship and practicality.

Special recognition to Rachel Halgarth and Joni Day, who unselfishly shared their time in organizing and editing the manuscript from its early stage. Thank you, guys.

ABOUT THE AUTHOR

Blessed M. Tamayo is an English second language speaker. Essay and poetry writing were his passion since his middle school grade. He came to the US with only $200 and a Word from the Lord through a dream; "I will send you to America for training and discipline." The Lord made good of His Word and favored Blessed to legally stay in the US and became an American citizen in the process.

In 2011, He completed his bachelor's degree in Information Technology Engineering at Charter College in Anchorage, Alaska. Such education became instrumental in harnessing his passion for creative writing. Looking back, he now fully grasps that going to a college system in America was part of God's dealing with him.

At three o'clock in the morning of the winter of 2011, the Lord woke him up and spontaneously flashed before him the 3 John 2 scripture. After reading it for several times, the Spirit of God unveiled the said scripture to him in a way that he has not seen it before, and then the Lord directed him to write this book – Breaking to Breakthrough.

He graduated from Antioch Faith Bible Training Center in 1984 with an emphasis in Global Mission. From 1984 to 1995, Blessed Tamayo pastored several small churches in the Philippines. He was also a frequent speaker to several Catholic Charismatic groups in Metro Manila and Bicol province.

He currently works as a Designated Service Engineer for Shell Oil Products US (SOPUS) in Texas. He is married for more than 31 years to Josie Tamayo, and they have two sons - Joshua and Ezekiel.

FOREWORD

This book reminds us of the great message that Jacob received from the LORD regarding the heavenly ladder (Gen.28:11-13). We as a leader must not stop growing in our spiritual stature in Christ. As King David said in Psalm 84:7; we must "…go from strength to strength." To take this spiritual stagnancy down, church's leaders today must need to experience new spiritual breakthroughs. Gospel ministers today need to experience what David declared, "The LORD has broken through my enemies before me like the breakthrough of water" (2 Sam.5:20). We need to break through the hindrances the devil placed in our paths in order to prevent us from drinking in the "well of GOD" (2 Sam.23:15-16); that is producing growth in our salvation (Phil.2:12) that supplies growth in our leadership life.

"Breaking To Breakthrough" is a timely book for every church leader who desires to get out of the "spiritual blindness" and "spiritual prison and shackles" that confines us to activities rather than separating us from the usefulness of our gifting and callings (Judges 16:21). By the grace of GOD, this SPIRIT-sent book will ignite a deep and genuine desire for spiritual breakthroughs.

Pastor Blessed Tamayo powerfully pointed out that fresh revelation from the depths of the Father's heart is the key to experience true freedom in Christ; fresh revelations catapults us to a place where God's greatness is tasted and seen.

HALLELUJAH! Expect your breakthrough as you go through the precious pages of this book.

Arnel Manalang
Touch of the Holy Spirt Church International
Founder/Overseer

OVERVIEW
Breaking Your Way to Breakthrough
To break is through

What Does God Got Ourselves Into?[1]

More likely, this abovementioned inquiry is what Paul and Silas were asking themselves after they get thrown in a Macedonian jail. It must have been soul-searching scrutiny where all sorts of conflict must have been played out in his mind as the Apostle compared their imprisonment to the vision the Holy Spirit showed him in Troas a few days back. Likely, He must have argued within himself; "this can't be a divine intention turned bad!" It is indeed an issue that collided head-on against their conviction in Christ.

Certainly, until we slip our feet into their shoes so to speak, we only somewhat understand the extent of their decisive experience. If you are in Paul's position, what is your take on the salinity of your sweat aggravating your back wounds caused by the Roman's whipping? Can you shun the temptation of second-guessing yourself? Is it worth it coming to Macedonia with the Gospel of Christ then ending up with these pain and chains? Apostle Paul may have said this; "Come on Silas, tell me; what is wrong with delivering a girl from an evil spirit in the name of Jesus?"

Vision: Conviction for our Mission Completion

When we seemingly lost our bearings, God's wisdom can guide us to evaluate our previous path. It seems coherent to say that the Apostle Paul most likely reminisces on the vision that he received from the Holy Spirit, where he saw a man who pleaded him to; "come over to Macedonia and help us."

Amid such a grim situation, he must have been convincingly saying these to himself; "God must have something in mind why we are here in this city!" Besides, that warden right there outside our cell is the same guy the Holy Spirit showed me in the vision!"

He perhaps argued; "no, this persecution is not the entirety of our Macedonian gospel story! It is just an episode of the whole narrative where Silas and I can realize the purpose of God for this season.

Ultimately, Paul and Silas' pursuit of their divine-given revelation resulted into the salvation of souls and the founding of the Macedonian church. Of course, such revival will not be realized without going through the said incarceration.

Through the years of acquaintance with the Holy Spirit's undertaking, these Apostles understood that what braces their God's assignment is the divine-given process that weaves in details of the mission's operation.

What conveys our soul's character are our responses or reactions to our given situation. With that in mind, we now understand that at the exasperating midnight hour Paul and Silas' resounding thanksgiving and praise gave evidence of their relationship with Christ; their priority of offering God of their uncommon worship gave a significant testimony about who the Lord Jesus is to them.

Indeed, they kept all inmates awake by their loud singing and prayers. The passion of their worship of God verifies that the spirituality of their faith is greater than the cloud of darkness that tries to constrict them.

The Holy Spirit's reason behind their incarceration was larger than themselves and bigger than their circumstances.

So, by breaking forth with songs of deliverance, God broke them through into the realm of the miraculous. More often than usual, when there is no going around life's impossible situation, the mindset of gratitude towards God is what can get us through our trials and testing.

When by revelation we passionately pursue God's revealed plan, our identity in Christ catapults us to the realization of our destiny.

Heaven Collides with Earth through Revelation

God fearsomely demonstrated His power when in worship Paul and Silas became a door where the Lord streams His divine purpose. Faith is the revelation of God's mind that enables us to connect our earthly situation with God's divine purpose.

Without revelation, there is no path for spiritual breakthrough. Without revelation truth, we cannot have an earthly experience of the spiritual God. Without the truth, we cannot genuinely worship God in the spirit.

When the Lord flowed through Paul and Silas' open hearts, His glory shook the whole prison system with a centralized earthquake and kicked the demonic stronghold out of that joint. The Lord miraculously broke all chains that bound them and opened all doors that barred them.

Yes! When God's presence shows up; everything that restricts us will be crushed. When amidst the difficulty, we choose to magnify God, the seemingly temporary sentenced of defeat will be swallowed up by Christ's resurrection life.

Nothing can hold us down when Daddy God shows Himself around. Situations change when God comes into our case.

Shaken and overwhelmed by an out of this world experience, all the prisoners never even thought of escaping but chose to remain where they are at. When the warden considered that he is as good as dead and supposing that all inmates had already escaped; Paul prevented him from plunging his sword against himself by telling him "we are all here!" Indeed, when God's wonders and signs accompany our faith declaration; our word elevates to an extraordinary importance.

In token of God's leading and guidance, all trails blaze to further the process until we realize His purpose. We cannot have a consummated breakthrough without going through a divinely administered course of action. Our spiritual leaping forward and the manifested presence of God go hand in hand. The birth of God's work in Macedonia resulted in such a way.

Above All Things

Beloved, I wish above all things that thou mayest prosper and be in health, even as thy soul prospereth.

3 John 2 KJV

At precisely 3 a.m. in the winter of 2011, the Lord woke me up. Then, out of nowhere, John's Third Epistle and the second verse spontaneously flashed before me. I quickly got up, sat on my bed, turned my computer on, and for several times I read the given passages.

Suddenly, these five words; "I wish above all things" breathed eternity into my awareness as the unexpected glimpse of light shines in the eye of my understanding. The eternal weight of glory that came along with such insight was so unspeakably overwhelming; I felt something shifted within my spirit. Truly, revelation distinguishes our connection with God.

There are two things that we must see to capture the spiritual understanding of these words; "I wish above all things." First, are the words "all things"; secondly, the statement "above all things." We must understand that these are two different life's position and condition. "All things" represents an ordinary life and "above all things," epitomizes an extraordinary life that resulted from a spiritual breakthrough or an outcome of divinely appropriated life.

In the process, I quickly double checked the insight that I received from God with the Greek Lexicon. The word "above" is the Greek translated word "peri" – from the root word "peran," meaning to "pierce through" (as adverb or preposition).[2]

It signifies an image of crossing —beyond, farther or (other) side, over. Therefore, the words "above all things" simply mean breaking or piercing through the usual "all things" unto the other side of "above all things."

An unspeakable joy of the Spirit overwhelms me for the second time, when Greek scholars confirmed the spiritual revelation that God showed me. Again, I jumped out of my bed and sang praises to the Lord in the spirit. It was an experience beyond a human description. When I came back to bed, I felt led to commence writing this book.

Our heart is God's portal of His heaven and His will on earth. What keeps the realm of God from manifesting His divine glory on this world is our soul's spiritual condition. We cross over to the side of God's supernatural realm when His truth prospers our soul.

Our soul is a go-between; it can be a spiritual or a carnal-driven persona. We can yield our mind, emotion, and will to God's will or we can settle to surrender it to our selfish desire. The heart of the matter is that we can breakthrough "above all things" or we can breakdown to the mediocrity of "all things."

Spiritual growth is not our recreated spirit progressing in spirituality, but it is our soul growing into the understanding and revelation of our position, identity, and destiny in Christ. As far as our recreated spirit in Christ is concerned, we are already complete in Him- who is the Head of all principality and power.

In the spirit, we are already the righteousness of God in Christ. We cannot get more righteous than that![3] The one that needs spiritual growth is our soul's understanding of who we are in Christ. When we allow the revelation of the Holy Ghost's invades our soul, then we become a living sacrifice persona for Christ; we turned into a living soul for God, ready to enforce God's dominion on the earth.

Our Earthly Spiritual Breakthrough

There are obstacles that hold back our soul from realizing our heaven on earth. To engage the reality of God's eternity on our temporal world, the ferocity of faith must aggressively enforce the claim of God's dominion over our soul.[4]

By putting everything in perspective, breaking through into the fullness of God's intention for our lives has a lot to do with breaking the corruptions and strongholds that are glaring our minds, curbing our emotion, and dominating our will.[5]

Self-preservation and self-entitlement are claims and sentiments of the flesh that obstruct us from externally and practically manifest who we are in Christ in the spirit. Self (or [fles]- the reversal of the word "self") always stands in God's way.

In the natural, prospects of the future may seem very intimidating, but we can always break to breakthrough via the sufficiency of God's grace within us. The grace of God which works within us both to do and to will is the catalyst where we can realize the plan of God for our earthly lives.

Our soul's transformation relates with our mind renewal. When the mind of Christ crushes the restricting strongholds of our soul, then there is nothing that can hold back the Holy Spirit from fashioning our souls unto a living persona for God.

We dismantle all opposing strongholds that are taking residence in the promise land of our souls through God's revelation and our yielding to Holy Spirit's direction.[6]

To manifest heaven on earth, our will must agree with the will of God. As we allow our minds to be invaded with God's spiritual truth, our life will manifest and personify God's eternal life and divine order.[7]

When we soaked in the presence of God and His Word, there is nothing that life's circumstance can squeeze out of us but the anointing of the Spirit and the revelation of God's Word.

God's Realm Converging into our Natural World

Beloved, I wish above all things that thou mayest prosper and be in health, even as thy soul prospereth.

3 John 2 KJV

God cannot be taken by surprise in any ways, shapes, and forms. He is the Alpha and Omega. He is the beginning, the end, and all the in-betweens.

When we set out our faith to venture on God's purposes, we may seem that we hit a roadblock. For God however, He already got acquainted with the finality of the whole thing before the end reaches its concluding climax. He knows everything! No one and nothing can surprise the Almighty. We, on the other hand are within the framework and processes of time and space. Therefore, relying on God who knows everything makes life exhilarating and exciting.

Spiritual breakthrough must initially take place in our soul for us to get through unto the other side. Strongholds, idols, and residue of disobedience must be first pulled down, cast down, and brought into captivity before we can experience the reality of the other side.

God's eternal realm must overrun our temporal world. Frankly speaking, we are not the one waiting. The other side is the one waiting for our crossing over.

As far as our spirit is concerned, we have all got what Christ has crucified and resurrected for. Nevertheless, that position of identity will remain only as inward reality unless our soul transform by the renewal of our minds.

It is interesting to note that the compound word 'transform' is a combination of trans and form. "Trans" means to "cross over, pass through, and go beyond. The word "form" means shape. When you combined these two words, it literally tells us that our soul must crossover to the realm of where the likeness and image of our recreated spirit in Christ is found and established.

Like Paul and Silas, we must crossover to the other side by imposing our God given revelation, our divine calling, and God's purpose over or on top of our trying circumstances.

As we invite His presence amidst our circumstances, Christ's new cosmos overwhelms our earthly chaos.

Embracing God's Process of Breakthrough

The spiritual breakthrough in the Body of Christ's falls in three phases; they are in order of the new birth of our spirit, the restoration of our soul, and the redemption of our mortal bodies.

These stages of breakthrough correspond with the stretch of our earthly existence because they affect our interaction with the past, the present, and the future. Understanding these three phases of spiritual breakthrough provides us the snapshot of our destiny's pathways.

Through God's revelation, our present can rightly relate with our past; when it does, we propel our identity to the realization of our destiny in the future. Understanding our consecration sequence as a triune being (spirit, soul, and body) is fundamental to the appropriation of our purpose and calling.[8]

The proper perspective regarding God's program for the wholeness of the entire man is indispensable to our relationship with God and with our fellowman. Such view is vital to our lifestyle of faith, crucial to our ability to rightly divide the Word of Truth, and vital to our discernment of God's voice.

The rebirth of our spirits in God's kingdom is our initial spiritual breakthrough. The new birth is all eternal and instantaneous divine spiritual experience. However, what God initialized in our spirit must also extend to our soul (mind, emotion, and will). The spiritual transformation of our soul outfits us with a living persona that connects with heaven and manifests its glory on earth.

A mind saturated with the revelation of the life of God enforces Heaven's dominion on the earth. Like Adam, we can operate in our God-given authority when we become a living soul. Only the meek - the teachable - inherits the earth.

Unlike the rebirth of our spirits which is instantaneous, our soul's transformation goes through an on-going transitional breakthrough. Soul-wise, we daily go through the process of spiritual sanctification. Fundamental understanding of this truth should not slip away from us regardless of progressive biblical teaching around us.

Finally, at the coming of our Lord Jesus Christ; in the twinkling of an eye, God will break our bodies through from corruptible unto immortal.[9] The rebirth of our spirit in the past and the redemption of our mortal body in the future are all 100% handiwork of God.

The breaking through of our faith to become who we are in our soul with who we already are in our spirit is the result of God co-laboring with His man and such breaking through is progressive.[10] It is the process of faith, grace, and glory (from faith to faith, from grace upon grace, and from glory to glory). The current Holy Spirit's work in our lives is all about our soul's conversion from self-consciousness unto God's consciousness.

The Divine Destiny of our Soul

> *Whom having not seen you love. Though now you do not yet see Him, yet believing, you rejoice with joy inexpressible and full of glory, receiving the end of your faith—the salvation of your souls.*
>
> *1 Peter 1:8-9 NKJV*

Receiving the finish line of our faith is the divine destiny of our soul. In Heaven, we will see the Lord Jesus Christ face to face; we will know Him just as much as we are known of Him. Therefore, we do not need faith and hope in heaven. Hope as well as faith ends here on earth, for these virtues deal with the unseen world.

The pulpit has been discounting the soul as the nemesis of our faith. No! The enemy of our spirit is the flesh, and they resist each other on the battleground of our mind. If by the grace of God through faith, we kept our soul single-minded on Jesus, our ways will be stable. Learning and realizing the yoke of the Master is where our soul can find rest.[11]

Our recreated spirit is already one with God's spirit. Our divine mandate on earth is to have our soul become one with our born-again spirit.

Our goal is to have our mind, emotion and will become united with our new creation spirit where the new man of the spirit become the core of our mind, bearing the image of God in true holiness and righteousness. In such state, the sword of the Word can no longer separate the spirit from the soul, for they come to the state of oneness.

The Three Manifesting as One

The New Covenant emphasizes three spiritual movements for the corporate church, as well as for the individual believers. They are from faith to faith, from glory to glory, and from grace upon grace. Faith and glory are an onward movement, one that leads to the other. Grace is an ascending movement; it is one on top of the other.

Faith is the revelation of the Father to Abraham. God's glory is the outshining knowledge of the Holy Spirit in the Church. Grace is the revelation of the Son to the world.

As we grow in faith and continue to experience more of His glory, we flourish in the liberating grace of our Lord Jesus Christ.

Today, there is a specific camp in the Body of Christ that emphasizes on the glory of God and manifestations of the Spirit are being seen in their gatherings. They are also those who highlight on the grace of God, declaring the Gospel of Christ – who is the Life and the Person of Jesus within us. Lastly, they are those who underscore the lifestyle of faith that pleases the Father; these are the ones who focus on the integrity of the Word.

God's course of spiritual movement never deviates, it stays. If somehow, we think these headways are just another doctrinal trend where we can hype ourselves up, then we are seriously mistaken.

In these last days, the combination of these three movements merging into one will release the greatest manifestation of the Godhead that we have never seen before. God's fullness is released from faith to faith, from glory to glory, and from grace upon grace.

The Core Intention of this Book

What confronts us nowadays is not the need for knowledge but the call to manifest what we already know. We realize our freedom in Christ when the truth that we are aware of is conveyed and understood in the level of experience.

Ideas that we formulate through information can easily be forgotten but the truth imprinted on our soul by a spiritual encounter with the Spirit of God is altogether life changing.

The central premise of this book is all about our soul's breaking out unto the fullness of Christ's image. As you read on through this book, be aware that every time the word "us" is mentioned, it often refers to our soul and not to our recreated born-again spirits.

On a personal note, laced on passages of this manuscript are scriptures that I elected not to mention. It is intentionally designed this way so that you will have the opportunity of letting the Holy Spirit puts you in remembrance of every scripture that He already personally revealed to you.

It is my utmost recommendation that you take notes and journal the things that God will personally share to you as you read this book. My prayer to the Father is that you will discover more of your eternal significance in Christ.

CHAPTER ONE
Launching Pad for Breakthrough
Breakthrough is a collaboration of God and man.

Launching Pad of the Supernatural

Back in 1984, the first church that I was privileged to lead conducted a three nights healing and evangelistic crusade. As we rolled into our second night, numbers of sick people responded to the altar call. A woman with a thyroid ailment asked me to pray for her condition. Her persistent plea put me on the spot and exposed my hidden insecurities. As I looked around and complained within myself, "How come I got this case when there are minor ailments around that can be easily tackled in prayer?! Besides, I never had an experience praying for such case."

Overwhelmed by the severity of her disease, my first human reaction as a neophyte in the ministry was to direct her to my spiritual father - Owen Baker. However, she told me that Papa Baker already prayed for her on the first night of the healing crusade. Her persistence to be prayed over left me no option but to go at it. Besides, the rest of the team was busy praying for the sick.

Right away, all my enthusiasm shrunk as if somebody must have set the panic button off. Fear was creeping in, and the silent thought of doubt was seemingly screaming with an eardrum-shattering voice, "What if nothing happens right after you prayed for her? For certain, you will be a laughingstock in front of these people!" Such thought of unbelief amplifies the feeling of awkwardness that I was already struggling on the inside. Seriously! My pride and self-preservation tried to escape, but there was no place to hide.

During this ensuing spiritual conflict, a soft spontaneous inner voice from within, wrapped up with so much love and unquestionable authority flooded and enlightened my heart; "Why do you worry so much? Is it you who will heal her?" Right away I realized that Jesus is the Healer and not me; I was exposed and convicted. In faith in the name of Jesus, I began praying for her healing and commanded the goiter to leave her throat.

Guess what? To my surprise when I opened my eyes, that nasty stuff was still hanging by her throat! However, something happened within me as soon as I saw that goiter, I felt like I grew bigger, bolder, and angrier with that disease. Like a river, the Holy Spirit's gift of faith flowed from within. I took her by the hand, and we walked towards where the microphone was standing. I said, "Here is the mic, take it, and testify to these people what the Lord has done for you." When I turned around and gave her the mic, I saw her in tears and being overwhelmed with the healing presence of Christ. God's miracle manifested as we were walking towards where the microphone stand was. Hallelujah! Glory to God!

We can do much, but our much is not always enough. The recognition of our limitations always greets us at our end. Nevertheless, when man's ability winds-up, the kickoff of God's sufficiency cranks up. Hanging out at the edge of our side of the bargain is not enough. Faith must take its stand and declare Jesus' redemptive authority until our condition in the natural world is broken through.

Self-determination is man's response to his ability in mounting up things that he wants to accomplish for God. Conversely, in God's kingdom, our responsibility must solely be our response to His ability alone. To crack down the impossible, the supernatural God must have a natural launching pad to unleash His compelling testimony.

Breakthrough is collaboration between God's inexhaustibility and man's limited capability. If we want God to execute the breaking of the impossible; it is our task to implement the doable. God's side of the bargain is to manifest the reality of His virtue; ours is to stand in agreement with His Word and engage it in faith. To break the unknown into the open, we must be willing to breach the impossible all the way with our God-given faith of the moment!

What breeds the thing that you can develop in your life has a lot to do with the environment that you get yourself settled. Just like Abraham, he left Ur for the land of Canaan which God promised him. By the same token, you must exit the environment that restricts you. Abandon the atmosphere of the ordinary and be willing to go where God wants you to go, and be what God wants you to be and have what God wants you to have.

With regards to the condition of our soul, there are things beyond who we are, what we have, and what we can do right now. There is more to our soul than its current spiritual condition. The discomfort of the unknown is not an acceptable alibi where we suspend ourselves in propelling to God's purposes. Where you have been through has no determination in realizing your destiny, but where God's Spirit is taking you.

Discover and capture the glimpse of where God is leading you! As we leap forward toward the new heights of faith, we will come to recognize that our soul's truest completion is waiting for us on the other side. Such soul's spiritual growth is always outside the confines of the ordinary.

We must go "above all things" instead of staying in the mediocrity of "all things."[12] Unless the reality of what's inside of us has its external manifestation, our righteousness position in Christ within our spirit is only partially realized. Unless we crack down the impossible, the world can expect nothing from us.

Pulling down carnal dispositions that restrict our mind from realizing our potentials in Christ is imperative to our soul's spiritual breakthrough. Indeed, we manifest what we believed we already are. Transitioning into such faith will not come unless the Lord opens and seals our ears with His instruction. Faith comes by hearing and hearing the voice of the Spirit of God.

Contentment is our disposition in life. The scripture teaches us to, "…be content with what we have."   The question is what do we have or rather who do we have? We can all say in unison of faith; "We have Christ the hope of glory within our spirit." Then if we have Him, can we ask for more when He is more than all?

Ironically, from our soul's standpoint, there will always be an incessant discontentment until we fully realized who we are in Christ. Until then, our soul will constantly yearn to breakthrough from glory to glory, from faith to faith, and from grace upon grace.

CHAPTER TWO
The Pathway to Breakthrough
What breaks self-dependency is God's supremacy

Brokenness: A New Covenant Principle

> *For though we walk in the flesh, we do not war according to the flesh. For the weapons of our warfare are not carnal but mighty in God for pulling down strongholds, casting down arguments and every high thing that exalts itself against the knowledge of God, bringing every thought into captivity to the obedience of Christ,*
>
> *2 Corinthians 10:3-5 NKJV*

The Controversy

Some sector of the Body of Christ deemed brokenness as pointless and unacceptable Christian dogma. They viewed such belief as the one that undermines Jesus' redemptive sacrifice. Of course, such confusion was a result of the denominational pulpit that spiritualized suffering through religious thinking. Consequently, they tossed the New Covenant's liberating principle into the muddy water of man's tradition.

For the most part, the said unbending censorship seems like justifiable, but the question that confronts us is "can we have a spiritual breakthrough without breaking the stronghold that restricts us?" Nowadays, when someone talks about brokenness, what comes to mind right away is the doctrine of spirituality through sickness, poverty, and death. What a shame!

Jesus said, "...if you being evil knows how to give good gifts to your children, how much more your Heavenly Father?"[13] We should not blame God as an evil authoritarian who teaches His people a lesson or two through hurtful means.

How can you make sense of God being a good Father, if sickness, poverty, and death are His prime measures of teaching us? Not to mention, Jesus came into this world to destroy the works of the evil one - the one who represents sickness, poverty, and death.[14]

There is no way that we can coin suffering as the source of our spirituality. Only God is the supply of good and perfect gifts. These accursed 'impairments' was brought by the devil into our world through Adam's disobedience. It is a contradiction in terms to even suggest that poverty, sickness, and mishaps are God's way of improving us spiritually.

This world should have been perfected by now if suffering is the factor that develops our relationship with the Father. Right? No! This planet has no shortages of suffering to go around if that is the case. Nonetheless, despite the gravity of suffering this world is known for, morality is still on the downward spiral decline. Apparently, our soul's transformation does not progress in such a way.

Don't you think that this misdirected notion is a false representation of the truth? This kind of sense can never be sensibly common! It is a double standard. We can be sincere with certain convictions; nevertheless, sincerity apart from the truth is misleading. Much ignorance emerges because truth is still elusive or not yet fully understood.

Life's situation gives rise to our opportunity to prove God and His Word is true. Life's challenges are occasions where our faith becomes relevant in breaking our true freedom in Christ through. How we respond or react to our given situation in life proves what manner of man we are.[15]

What Brokenness is NOT

The New Covenant principle of brokenness is not a process of spiritual development through sickness, poverty, and death. To be broken with the things that Jesus once and for all suffered in His vicarious cross is nothing but a purpose defeating rhetoric.

On the cross, Jesus negated every ill effect of Adam's rebellion by trading His fullness for our emptiness.[16] The benefits of Jesus' brokenness on the cross are for our good and not for our loss. For our sake, the death that Jesus suffered on the cross enables us to share the triumph of His resurrection. He became one with us so that we can become one with Him.

No one can take His life away from Him; Jesus can only lay it down. Adam's disobedience brought the reign of sin and death into the world; Jesus' obedience unto death and sin is the price that undoes it.

Adam was born again into death nature of the devil by disobedience. However, our spirit's regeneration in God's Kingdom was made possible through the obedience of Christ unto His spiritual separation from God.

With the intention of delivering our soul from sin which still the residual system of this present evil age, Jesus willingly gave up His life for us according to the will of God.[17]

The price has been paid off. Jesus nailed down God's plan of redemption completely complete and utterly perfect. Our faith can now declare that all the curses that we inherited from Adam were all that Jesus broke off at the cross.

His brokenness at that vicarious tree is all that we were all made complete and lacking nothing. The curse that He died for us all is the blessing that we are now privileged to enjoy.

What Brokenness IS

An element of deliverance is put into effect each time our soul spiritually breaks through. We leak out the new cosmos of Christ into our worldly chaos when carnal restrictions (strongholds) are broken off.

Without a barrier to traverse, the Holy Spirit's creative solutions has no opportunity to emerge. The setback is not what it seems it is; our soul cannot crossover unto the other side without an impediment to pierce through.

Brokenness is breaking our soul's insufficiency with Christ's all-sufficiency. What breaks self-dependency is God's supremacy. On our recreated spirits, God already engraved His provision for our soul's restoration.

Our Heavenly Father has foreordained this inscription of good works within the depth of our being. It is His will for us to walk on the revelation of His gospel of Christ (His life, His death, and His resurrection).[18]

To rendezvous with our destiny in Christ, understanding brokenness in the light of the New Covenant truth is essential. What needed to be exposed is the stronghold of a wrong belief system that is still residing in our minds.

God's revelation of His goodness links us up to access His divine provision. We cannot have the revelation of God without having His rich and abundant supply. Through His revelation His kindness is verifiable on all facets of our earthly existence.

Without the revelation of God's redeeming love, savoring His awesome favor is beyond our reach. The revealed will of God enables our mind, emotion, and will for us to keep in step with the Spirit of God. In the simplest way of putting it, we reflect the truth that enlightened us, and we resonate our divine encounter with God.

Correct believing coupled with the Holy Spirit's anointing settles a Jesus lifestyle. A conviction that resulted from a revelation leads to rewarding expressions. Like Noah of old, we will vanquish any deluge of oppositions, when we let God's Spirit guides us. The revelation and the anointing of the Holy Ghost is what break the idolatry in our minds, will, and emotions.

Our Entry is Our Exit

> *That ye put off concerning the former conversation the old man, which is corrupt according to the deceitful lusts; And be renewed in the spirit of your mind; And that ye put on the new man, which after God is created in righteousness and true holiness.*
>
> *Ephesians 4:22-14 KJV*

Our spiritual leaping forward from one level to the next is an ongoing process. The scripture puts it this way; we live from faith to faith, transformed from glory to glory, and reign in life from grace upon grace. Each level of encounter leads to subsequent spiritual assignment.

Do not get surprised to realize that we are just getting started again on the different elevated levels whenever we suppose that on our last go-around we already culminated. As we grow in the Kingdom of God, we experience the grace of the Lord stacking up one after the other.

Every exit door in God's Kingdom is passed through the new entry door. Every revelation that we engaged and completed is walked out through the door of faith's new assignment. Our life in the Kingdom of God is a constant going out and coming in. The latter prospect of glory is where we transitioned the former. The new is the exit from the old.

Breakthrough from our side of the view is going over, but from God's side of the view, it is where we are coming-over. It is revealing when we flip the word; breakthrough is nothing more but a manifestation of an "overcoming" life; experiencing the settled truth of God's blessings that awaits us on the other side.

Each thrust of our soul's spiritual breakthrough is a juncture where the deal of demolishing heights of arrogant attitude that is in defiance of the true knowledge of God happens. On our faith's respective season, rivers of God's glory flow unrestrained when a present self-restriction in our soul is broken-off.

The currency for the earthly manifestations of the Kingdom is a living sacrificed body separated for the plan and purposes of God. Of course, through soul's restoration, these can be done.[19] Each stage of our soul's spiritual breakthrough comes with a new expression of anointing. Such spiritual shift in the Body of Christ comes with an anointed song which resonates true spiritual freedom.

Self-denial or putting off the old man is not an account of defeat; it is a life's gain because Jesus is given an occasion on our lives to reign. Christ honored Stephen with standing ovation when he gave his life for the sake of the Gospel. When our earthly life come into agreement with His will, God validates us with an open-heaven experience.

The more our soul considers its death to self-consciousness, the more we open ourselves up to God's authority. The more we draw nigh to Him, the more He draws Himself nigh to us.[20]

We must shun from human insistence to merit holiness, let us rather welcome the fullness of what Jesus already provided. By way of practical experience, His proximity spells out the authority of His presence over us, and when He is near us, the devil and his miserable deception is basically away from us.

Our Father in heaven is eager to see that soul's self-consciousness is completely get out of the WAY, out of the TRUTH, and out of the LIFE. Until we lose our self-dependency, we cannot practically gain the blessings of God's supremacy.

The heart where Jesus lords over is a life where His actual territory is. The place where Jesus rules as Lord is an impregnable life against all oppositions and enemies. At the other side, God and His divine intention are waiting for our soul's spiritual crossing over.

Breaking Out from our Own Isaacs

Inherent within our recreated spirits is the eventuality of our divine destiny, and it is contingent to our soul's enlightenment on who we already are in Christ. No one gives more glory to the Father than a man who because of the touch of God shifted the gear of his divine calling to full throttle surrender.

The offering of our body as a living sacrifice is our response to our view of His mercy and it should not in anyways be treated as a religious penance. However, if you choose to keep your personal Isaac as an idol, then such decision then your life's God given purpose is ditch by the wayside.

Directed between yourself and your breakthrough is the offering of your own personal Isaac. Such submission decides the culmination of the full display of your inheritance in Christ.

When what we believe is expressed in action, the result is what we called the faith's realization. You see faith must initially be heard and received, then believe in the heart and confess with the mouth, acted upon, manifests in the natural, and impart to your fellowman. Reversing this priority of order always terminates to delusion and confusion.

Losing your prized pride hurts. There is no redemption for self but death. Nevertheless, the temporal comfort of self-preservation cannot even come close to the reward of our fulfilled eternal destiny in Christ.

What we must now sacrifice on the altar of God is the wounded ego that we have been indulging for the longest of time. Using the eternal stretch of God's grace to rationalize a sinful lifestyle can no longer be acceptable on all fronts; we mostly use it as an excuse because we still enjoy sin's worldly stimulation.

Letting go of a cherished and prized possession is unparalleled because such surrender conveys the pain of separation. The surrender of our Isaac precedes to the tearing down of the stronghold of self-entitlement. Such abandonment is an opening for God to launch His purpose.

The giving part and its benefits has been established by God, and what remains to be seen is the receiving part of it. The renewed mind that offers self as a living sacrifice verifies how good, acceptable, and perfect the will of God is.

Angels are clueless about the joy of forgiveness and restoration, and yet they participate with the joy that the heart of the contrite one releases.[21] It completely throws them off in awe of God when His forgiveness connects earth with heaven. The release of the angelic celebration in God's presence is tied up with the aura of the eternal weight of joy reflected on the faces of the contrite ones.

From the side of eternity, angels are constantly keeping an eye on the repentant ones as they turn to God. Angels respond to an aura of veneration that rises to God's throne when a repentant mind decides a body offering that emits an acceptable and a sacrifice of a sweet aroma of worship.[22]

'Nothing' Can but 'Some-One' Could

> *I am sure that NOTHING separate us from God's love – not life or death, nor angels or spirits, nor the present or the future, not powers above or the powers below. Nothing in all creation can separate us from God's love for us in Christ Jesus our Lord!*
>
> Romans 8:38-39 CEV

It is important to note that every entity, condition, power, and influence mentioned by Paul in Romans 8:38-39 are all personified as "NOTHING!" God the Father singled them all out as incapable of separating us from His enfolding love.

Remarkably, Romans 8:38-39 pointed everything and everyone out except the self. The one who can defy the purposes of God is neither the devil nor the channels which are or who are at his disposal.

The entitlement of self is the only ground on which the enemy can cling and continually oppose God's plan for our lives. We stand in the way of God when we choose our way better than God's will. It is not that complicated! When we are fascinated with our self-preservation, heaven is tied up until the revelation of the truth sets our soul free.

In matters of releasing God's settled intention, heaven indeed is the one waiting for those who are on the earth. Man's agreement with the settled will of God is what makes us realized heaven in this world.

There should be a surrender of self and acceptance of the only Way – Jesus. For all and eternity He has already made His move through Jesus' death, resurrection, and ascension.

Now in regards with our soul, God is the One waiting for us to posture what Christ has already done and accomplished! In Heaven, everything that concerns our position in Christ is already a done deal, and every entity and elements that are antagonistic to our inheritance in Christ were already bound.

Our Heavenly Father is always ready to manifest Himself on our behalf. His time is always perfect in the present! The experience of His salvation is always in the now! Nevertheless, the spiritual condition of our soul delays us from catching up with the move of His Spirit. To be on the same playing field with Him, radical transformation of our soul is imperative!

Finding His life within us is the only way we will lose the hold of the old life. Self will break us down when we do not break out from the self. Life is this expressive. We fail when we do not let God's seed of success breaks from the inside out. We grow and refresh daily, or we dry as our soul spiritually thaw. Unless the seed is sown on the ground of our soul, our potential is not dynamically found.

Our testimony in our life's practicality manifests our enemy's defeat. What we break out to be is what we affect the world to see. We are the doer, and the Holy Spirit is our helper. Our participation with the Holy Spirit activates all that God represents for us in Christ in the here and now. Our lives were made to live out God's intention. Now is the time to shine as God's light of the world. Now is the occasion to become the catalyst of change. It is now the time to be the Word in the flesh. Do not delay; align your soul with God's revelation in the now.

Everything about who we are in Christ is a burden that is light and easy if it is employed in the recommended setting of Christ's grace. It is not by might nor by power but by the Spirit of God. For those who have the Spirit of God, everything is made known in plain view; it is all in the Word of God. Read it as it is, believe it as it is, say it as it is, and live it as it is.

Our life in Christ is not a doctrinal complication; it is our divine position to function. When we navigate life based on fleshly notions, uncertainty looms on the horizon. Destiny is what faith in God and His Word, substantiates. There is no need to experiment on sketchy curiosity just to discover what quenches our dehydrated soul. Jesus is our Living Water. Enough said!

God already revealed, established, and implied His grace. Heaven anticipates in seeing it applied. Again, it is a misconception to say that grace's expression is a state of spiritual living that God is the only One doing it all and human participation has no significance at all.

God gave us this physical body and ability to make choices for one reason; we must use our body and our mind for none other than our means of expressing His glory. Whether you like it or not, God planted us here on earth, so that we can be the fullness of His grace. We become the courier of His manifested glory when we let the Spirit of God work in us both to do and to will.

Breaking through our Gethsemane

> *So we are always confident, knowing that while we are at home in the body we are absent from the Lord. For we walk by faith, not by sight.*
>
> *2 Corinthians 5:6-7 NKJV*

> *For our light affliction, which is but for a moment, is working for us a far more exceeding and eternal weight of glory, while we do not look at the things which are seen, but at the things which are not seen. For the things which are seen are temporary, but the things which are not seen are eternal.*
>
> *2 Corinthians 4:17-18 NKJV*

The Gospel never mention Gethsemane as a garden. Gethsemane means "an oil press." Based on its ancient description, it was a place where olives are compressed to produce anointing oils for priest and kings. It is a significant place because Jesus frequently visits the place to pray.[23]

Gethsemane is a precursor to Calvary. It is where Jesus was hard pressed on every side: spiritually, physically, mentally, and emotionally. Crucifixion was just an outcome of Jesus' breakthrough in Gethsemane, where he passed through and overcame the vision of the cross' inevitable pain and agony.

Jesus went the extra mile for us. He turned the other cheek instead of judgment. He took our tunic of sin, so He can cloak us with His robe of righteousness.

These were as far as Jesus committed Himself in demonstrating God's redeeming love for humanity. What a love! For Him, we are worth it even though we do not deserve it. What an awesome grace!

The real temptation transpired in Gethsemane and not at Calvary. Jesus as a man struggled to contend with the will of the Father. He even implied that if there is another way for the great plan of redemption to undertake, He will go through that route. Nevertheless, He did not cut corners, but He walked right through it, Jesus walked right through it!

At that crucial moment where Jesus felt so alone, He was even tempted to rely on the strength of men. Jesus' repeated His appeal to Peter, James, and John to tarry with Him in prayer even for one hour, but it fell on their slumbering ears. Though emotionally burdened, nevertheless, He chose to drink His preordained cup of suffering.

The blood that He sweated on His forehead confirmed that He was agonizing on envisioning the horror of His pending sacrifice. The revelation of the awaiting anguish of His disconnection from the Father made Him think twice about carrying it out.

By breaking from His will in pursuit of the Father's will, His breakthrough in Gethsemane became His platform for His greatest sacrifice at Calvary. In the presence of His Father, Jesus separated Himself for the will of God. He knew that to take on God's plan of redemption, the only way through it is His brokenness.

The only thing that stood between God and His redemption of man was Jesus' obedience to the Father's will. Yes, though it will mean His spiritual disconnection from the Father, Jesus willingly drank the cup of suffering because He beheld the joy of our becoming – sons and daughters of the King!

In perspective, when we realize our limitation, we can venture on God's solution. Surprisingly, His solution for our breakthrough is often to go through. The important part of breakthrough is to go through. We will remain in our natural disposition in life unless we understand how to harness trials, testing, and temptation for our spiritual advantage.

Let me qualify this statement: Trials and temptations are not the basis for our breakthrough; they are just an opportunity where through faith and patience we process our God given revelation to precipitate the manifestation of our sonship.

The response of faith launches our soul's spiritual breakthrough; oppositely, our reaction of fear sold our soul up to breakdown.

The Kingdom of God is a series of breaking through. By continuously tapping on the ever-increasing dimension of God, this relentlessly enables us to walk with Him. Going through the process of brokenness spells out the forfeiture of our pricey carnal attachments.

What we coined the wrong that we feel right are our all-time hang-ups. Nevertheless, truth disregards complexions, status, and gender. What truth conveys mostly disagree with our baffled romanticized emotions. Seriously, truth hurts with extreme prejudice.

During such season of trials, God speaks to us by every available means. God the Father is telling us time and time again that our human ways will never work for us. Human strength will never have its fullness because flesh always winds down.

Tapping on the power of the Holy Spirit, however, gets us to the fullness that is beyond what we can imagine or think. Discerning the heart and the mind of God during the season of breaking our soul's stronghold sustains us to carry out the death sentence to self as well as the manifestation of the power of His resurrection in our lives.

Brokenness and breakthrough are the two sides of the coin. Our revelation of Christ's fullness breaks us through from our soul's self-consciousness unto walking on God's divine intention.

There is no such thing as middle ground in the plans and the purposes of God. Gray is not the color of the Kingdom. A walk of faith is a life of spiritual over the natural; it works out the ascendency of eternity over the temporary substitutes for His glory.[24] Strongholds that are illegally residing in our soul are broken through by the revelation of Christ's crucifixion and resurrection.

Fresh revelation oozes out renewed commitment. When God unveiled His heart towards the actual condition of our soul, such spiritual perception inspires and enables us to embrace His goodness; such understanding launches our mind to think God's thoughts and ways.

Mind you, divine revelation comes with supernatural ability to carry out God's will. Faith is our supernatural given ability to walk with our Father, and such ability comes when the Lord personally speaks His Word to us.

Resonating our Being in Christ

God's solution always precedes man's need. Because of man, the whole creation came into existence. They were all created by God to fill the need of man. On the other hand, God Himself is the sole reason why man exist.

God's plan is not a boring thing that we pursue in shadow; we are all designed to resonate God's purpose in the light. Man's identity is defined to the fullest when his relationship with God the Father extracts the eternity within his recreated spirit.

Since we first occurred in the Father's mind, God constantly dreamed of us reaching our calling of greatness. On earth, we are meant to be the exact representation of God and His heaven. Of course, this can only be made possible by Christ resurrection life manifesting through our lives.

You should've gotten' it by now, the Kingdom of God is all about His life, His Word, His Spirit, His ways, His thoughts, His mind, His plan, and His purpose. Through faith, we are just the living conduit of God's glory and grace. We go as He flow.

God's predisposed His eternity in our new creation spirit. Our soul can break through the casing of our carnal limitation when we let the Spirit of God invades our mind, emotion, and will.

Our soul is a go between the spirit and the natural world. God is released from our inner man unto this world when we become a living soul. Therefore, a personal encounter with God is not an optional privilege, but it is an unavoidable path.

Central to the celebration of our freedom in Christ is our soul's breaking out from its restriction. Without breaking off from our human predictability, crossing over unto Christ's immensity is unlikely. Between our side of the ordinary and God's supernatural eventualities are our divine ordained breakthroughs.

We and the world around us are most benefitted by our God-given calling when our soul spiritually breaks out. Something must be broken first to get us through unto the other side. Brokenness is the pathway to breakthrough. The only way to break is through!

God's eyes run to and fro between infinity and the world of temporary to seek for someone whose soul is totally at peace with Him. Such man is whom He will manifest His glory; a living persona who is totally sold out with the power of Christ's redemptive plan. Are you sold out with Christ's cross and resurrection?

God knew where you would exactly match with His plan; He arranged and placed you for such a time as this. You exist in this generation not because God knows that you need an iPhone but because your uniqueness has its place for this segment of human history. God deliberately fashioned you for this generation; you are the apple of His eye – the beneficial focal point of His eternal purpose.

When people have no idea where they should spiritually relate to, they are fragmented, oblivious, and inundated with a sense of emptiness. We have got to discover where we are in God's scheme of things. Impersonation can never make a difference. We have nothing to share when we are not giving from the resource of our gifting within.

We do not just exist to live. Our divine-given life in Christ defines our existence. Surviving is not living; living is breathing His life in continuous fashion. Life is not trying to live. We live to express Christ's being – our pearl of a great price from within.

Resounding His being this way is a far cry from stomaching mediocrity. Our acknowledgment of what our soul is lacking only points us to God's suitable solution - Jesus.

Our past's experience nor our future's supposed prospects are incapable of releasing our divine potential. Our key that unlocks our divine-given life is Christ – our ever-indwelling hope of glory.

Exaltation Precedes Submission and Humility

We cannot be petrified of the process because great nuggets of wise solutions can creatively emanate from the Holy Spirit within. Being in the presence of God amid the grind can turn up our sensitivity to God's creativity. Self-pity and self-centeredness can keep us from seeing things otherwise.

The kingdom of darkness concentrates all its effort in using our carnality to blind our minds from understanding who we are in Christ. The truth is whatever Jesus inherited as the Son is also ours. In Christ, God's greatness is vested within us.

Greatness is not a flicker of coincidence. In the grind, we manifest God's greatness when we quit standing in His way. Exaltation precedes submission and humility. What decides the fulfillment, or what delays our soul's destiny is on how we engage our lives during hostility. Do we engage it in faith or fear?

When you do not let go of your God-given dream, and you do not concede to temporary fixation that sooths your pain, you are on your way to engage your soul's destiny to completion. When it gets tough, do not negotiate your conviction of the real for some alternative deal.

...hold that fast which thou hast, that no man take thy crown.

Revelation 3:11 KJV

During the grinding season, when people scrutinize you and haplessly categorize you based on their perception of merit, this is nothing but adding more insult to injury. Mostly, such spiritual warfare is painful, lonesome, and it puts us in the brink of emotional stress. Indeed, you and God alone knows the intensity of the pressure and the compression of the resistance you are facing. Nonetheless, we can learn from the Holy Spirit to improvise and customize when we are being tempted to compromise.

Faith is audacious in carrying out impossible tasks. However, when everything is getting blurred, our focus can be adjusted by fine-tuning our heart's motivation. To clear our spiritual periphery, the crucial point is to discard the unnecessary. Clear prophetic vision will carry us through up to the end.

However, pain is a part of the process, we should not allow resentment to take the best of us though, we should let the process enlarge our heart's capacity and extend our understanding to receive God's best. We learn to love in unlovable situations. In losing ourselves for what God offers, we find ourselves hidden in the resurrection life of Christ.

Brokenness is not an end to itself; it is just part of the bigger picture. God does not want you to stay broken; He can take our brokenness and make our soul whole. Wholeness is the purpose of the brokenness of the soul.

Our mind, emotion, and will assume its allocated wholeness when our soul spiritually breaks through. Because of what the grace of God is capable of dispensing through us, we can rejoice knowing that in all things, God is our portion. God is our abundance amid deficiency.

CHAPTER THREE
Breaking unto Greatness
Greatness breaks through from the inside out

We Break Through from the Inside Out

From its reserved protein and water within its sheltered shell, a calmly pre-hatched eaglet nourishes itself to growth. While from the outside, its incubating parents provide its need for warmth, comfort, and protective connection.

As the eaglet rapidly grow, the reserved nourishment where it draws comfort and contentment considerably decreases. It then instinctively defaulted to breach the shell with its beak to set itself out free from its restrictive containment.

Eventually, the external light and its parent's scent pierced through the gaps of its ruptured shell, a newfound discovery intuitively fired-up its eagerness to breach its restricting casing twice as many as before.

With its renewed hope, it batters the shell with successive beatings until the crack splits in different directions. The breakages became an opening, and the opening became the eaglet's way of escape from its confining habitation.

The eaglet urgently screams its sense of freedom as it hastily burst itself out of the shell, and with excitement it squeaks to call out its parent's attention, touch, and provision.

Alas, it made it through onto the other side where the eagle's majestic upward soar with a grander view awaits the creature's sight. Truly, the sky will be its limit of flight.

In perspective, we are not designed to maintain the same level of grace, faith, and glory for the rest of our earthly life. From one stage of faith to the next height, the gospel continually reveals our righteous position in Christ.

By God's divine revelation our soul can break through from the inside out, spread the wings of our identity, and harnesses the wind of troubles for our advantage.

Life is not hard; they are just challenging and confrontational. As a new class of being in Christ, greatness is our bound destiny. The process of shattering the residue of the old nature that illegally resides within our conscious and subconscious mind is vital to our soul's spiritual breakthrough.

Certainly, earthly complications along the way are unavoidable. In many shapes and forms, deceiving obstructions will try to block our pursuit of God. What limits us is not how the world evaluates us, but how we regard ourselves during setbacks. Nonetheless, God Almighty will never quit seeing who we are in Christ, what we have in Christ, and what we can do in Christ. We need to see our God given life through His eyes and not through our missed opportunities.

Our existence is not determined by our past's impediments, for the grace of His cross and His resurrection fixed who we already are in Christ. You do not have to do anything to give yourself a pat on the back and patronize yourself. His grace is all there is for your secured identity.

It is human to appraise life based on the prescription of natural senses. However, to carry out our conviction in the manner of taking God at His Word is entirely divine.

Having our disposition taking its root from our past failure only defines our lives within its stipulated confinement, but through the Holy Spirit's divine-given revelation, our potential in Christ is launched, thus God can take us to places beyond our wildest imaginations.

What excludes us to the being of faith is the life that is exasperated by the feedback of sight. Faith eliminates fear. Living by sight, however, impedes the validation of our belief. Fear generates bondage, but faith releases us to who we already are in the Lord Jesus Christ.

Even when you are down and out in the natural, your only way is up when you allow the revelation of the Word and the Spirit sharpens your perspective.

Regardless of what happened in the past, our Heavenly Father sticks with His original plan. By His grace, He knows you will come around. His Plan-A fits us best. God does not make mistakes. He does not even have a plan-B contingent to the flaw of our humanity.

Nothing surprises our God the Father. Your sin nor your failure cannot startle Him. The good Lord has no intention of letting you exist here on earth without attaching His Plan-A with your life. You have never been an error in His eyes. The Father is waiting all these times for you to come along with His original plan.

The best is what God have you in mind! The time is always now for you to break out from all the apprehension of your carnal restrictions. Your soul's spiritual breakthrough is an element where you realize your true spiritual identity in Christ.

The Massive Potential of Small Beginnings

As the warm solar beams collide with moisture coming from the West Virginia's fertile orchards of Shenandoah Valley, the air vibrantly radiates the coming season of harvest.

These groves once started as an apple seed; now they are a testimony to the possibility of millions of apple fruits in its foreseeable lifetime or a probability of countless numbers of orchards.

Greatness always starts from its humble beginnings; the early stage of a success story should not be despised. In maturing our soul's spiritual stature, we must start from the beginning; like in climbing a ladder, we always start from the bottom step.

> *Though your beginning was small, yet your latter end would increase abundantly.*
>
> Job 8:7 NKJV

We cannot ignore small things; they are vital parts that bond great things together. Even down to the atomic level, God's principle of multiplication keeps on so that life's engagement can go on. Atoms, though maybe microscopic in size and invisible to the naked eyes, their impact is colossal. As microscopic as they can be, yet they hold the whole earth together as one. Everything that radiates life is multipliable to its highest level.

Philip mocked the initial and concluded it as final when he gauged the 5,000 men greater than the potential of five loaves of bread and two fishes on the hands of Jesus. Philip complained and said, "What are they among so many?"[25]

Living by the directives of the natural senses restricts us in unbelief, but God Almighty can do beyond what we can ask, dare imagine, and think.

Weighing our life's condition as overwhelming in comparison to our small beginnings will always cause us to be a pessimist. Rather, we can choose to believe that darkness potentially serves as a backdrop for the heavenly bodies to shine brighter.

When we understand that we only reflect the light that comes from the Sun of Righteousness, it is just a matter of time for Him to spread from within us the healing of His wings.

Only the radicals believe beyond the eyes of the skeptical. Nothing can stop us from pursuing our dreams when we start believing what we can do in Christ as opposed to our what we are restricted of due to our external circumstances.

God's solution and intervention are all written up in His scripture. His Word is the platform where we can see life through His perspective.

Our problem is an occasion point where we can start praying out the Father's divine viewpoints of us amidst all worldly contradiction. Prayer is standing in agreement with the Father to have His heaven extends on the earth.

When a man reached his end of the road, God's wisdom is just starting out to transcend. There is no hopeless case for God; they are only His opportunities where we can step it up in faith.

We always complain and say, "What I have right now is not enough to get me started." That is a lot of terrible lies! We must only be willing to start with what God has already invested within us. All you need is what God has given you, and by God's grace, you can precede it to a manifestation of victory.

All the ten lepers had, were just Words of Jesus; "Go show yourselves to the priest."[26] When they believed and acted correspondingly, they all got cleansed along the way. There are things that we set in motion when our faith stage it up in action.

Wake your potentials up from spiritual slumbering! Our destiny's authenticity will remain out-of-the-way unless we engage our purpose in full throttle.[27]

David and his stones were inconsequential in comparison to Goliath's size. The stone was all that David had, but when in faith he let go his insignificant weapon; it released all that God has for him.

When David became willing to face the giant with Whom he is and with Whom he can do things, the enemy got the beat down, and the influence of terror lost his head that day.

The extremist troublemakers who try to grip our nation in fear will be put to shame when we let go our natural insignificance to the hands of God Almighty. We will witness how God intervene in our lives when we engage life in such a way.

There are always two elements to a miracle: God's operation and faith's act of submission. He has already given; the receiving and acting part are all that what is left. We will never come to the grip of God's lasting and satisfying rewards when we keep on betraying ourselves with things that temporarily soothes our pain.

The uncommitted heart is the culprit behind an existence that spins in perpetual motion. In the flesh, to start is challenging because it presumes that it takes a costly commitment to fuel the fire.

When we crank things up in faith, what is left of us is the Holy Spirit's timely season to manifest the harvest of God's completed dream.

We cannot finish anything until we steadfastly believe in our God-given dream and allow the Holy Spirit helps us fuel our desire with His fire so we can cross over on the other side.

God has given us the grace to complete His purpose in our lives.[28] Our dream gets rewarded when by faith we hang on to it. Recognition of God's greatness within us inspires us to fight for what rightfully belongs to us.

Greatness Goes Beyond Self

We are truly vulnerable if we left on our own devices. The reality of challenges in life has a way of making us realize that we need a set of guiding eyes that perceive things beyond human capacity to distinguish. The plan of God written on the tablet of our hearts does not flow independently from the revelation and the anointing of the Holy Spirit.

The divine-directed path is beyond the reach of a self-contained person. Counting on God's ways of doing things is a light that makes the path of our life perceivable. The book of Proverbs says.

> *In all your ways acknowledge Him, and He will direct your paths.*
>
> Proverbs 3:6 NKJV

What would the world be if there is no oxygen? Everything will be lifeless, desolated, and dry. Oxygen is an element in the natural that we cannot live and do without. On the same token, taking God out of the equation, spirituality in its truest sense is not happening. We cannot just leave God on the sideline and then go ahead with our self-fabricated righteousness. Outside God's providence, we are spiritually blind and barren.

We undisputedly accept that our cars cannot run without combustible fuel. However, we always find all kinds of excuses when it comes to running our existence with the presence of God.

You must come to terms with the truth that you cannot have a relationship with just yourself alone. Our destiny is not foreseeable unless we find where we are divinely connected.

Greatness goes beyond self. True greatness comes only when we seek the greatness of God first. Everything that proceeds out of God's excellence culminates in the immensity of possibilities in this life and in the life to come.[29]

Our new life in Christ is designed to function efficiently with our relationship with God the Father. Religion is all we can put on the table so to speak if we try to make things on our own.

Even faith outside the love of God will not work. If charity is not self-seeking and it does not insist its way, then faith is not a tool where we can selfishly collect a manse of things so that we can parade to the whole world that our faith has done it all.

The grace of God that is apprehended and received by faith defines the reality of His great salvation in us. Consequently, our world's sphere of influence would happen to witness the greatness of God in our lives. Such testimony of God's goodness in our lives draws them to the light of the Kingdom.

Legalistic religion is a spinoff of spirituality outside God's goodness. The revelation of God's love is what balances faith.[30] Taking God's kindness out of our faith's declaration is pointless and empty. Just like a fish outside its liquid realm, life is suffocating without the favor of His goodness. Faith outside the virtue of God's love is imbalanced and inconsistent. Faith is beyond self-containment.

FOR God, faith has a directing and fulfilling purpose; WITH God, faith is the possibility of all things; THROUGH God, faith is alive, and it gives us the ability to separate the mediocrity from the abundant life that we already have in Christ.

Faith is not a label where we can pronounce what brand of spirituality we associated ourselves with. If we only seek to preserve our religious ticket more than the harmony and oneness that the love of God endorses, then our belief will not amount to anything, but we will be like a noisy gong or a clanging cymbal.

Faith is not self-imposition, it is not self-initiative, and it is not self-determination. Faith is the revelation of how God sees things. True faith is not blind, oblivious, and feeble minded. Outside God's wisdom, faith is a lifeless notion incapable of yielding divine influence and spiritual manifestation. Faith is the operation of God wherein we manifest His Kingdom and His will on earth.

Faith comes through hearing the Spirit of God in His Word. A faith that is a derivative of God's revelation is God's arm suited for every life's season. True faith inhale and exhale the greatness of God; it abandons fleeting things, and it procures eternal rewards.

We cannot stress faith more enough to say that such venture is beyond the reach of self. We build God's monument in our lives when we deny soul of self-consciousness and establishing his ticket to God out of self-righteousness. True faith is sticking with what Christ has already set for us.[31]

The Paradox of Greatness

The Kingdom of God, which is the reign of Jesus over us is all about giving and receiving; it is an all-time irony of dying and living. We always hear that salvation is free, and it is 100% grace. True! However, faith activates the supply of God's grace when we repent from dead works. Faith cannot go towards the ways of God without turning our back from the pointless religion of man. Apostle Paul said.

> ...repentance from dead works and of faith toward God...
>
> Hebrews 6:1 NKJV

Self always stands in the way of our faith walk. You see, Christ's life manifests when we die to self-entitlement. In demonstrating God's Kingdom, somebody must have to give in; the old man and new man cannot share the same playing field at the same time. We need to understand that repentance is our claim of death to our usual self and resurrection life is the manifestation of the active faith.

The relentless impact of faith and repentance personally hinges us with God's eternal plan for our lives. Having this insight helps us appreciate that faith and repentance build our soul's spiritual legacy.

Repentance is our present spiritual posture that deals with our past. On the other hand, faith is our present conviction that lays hold the unsubstantiated future; faith calls out the future as a God-verified fact in the present.

Our present initiative will be like a never-ending spin of commencing but void of mission completion when the past is left undone. Seriously, it will be an ever occurrence of the past popping its ugly head up whenever we are on the verge of putting the finishing touches for our divine assignments.

The unfinished business of the past will always sabotage our path moving forward. Securing our past and our future with the revealed will of God takes care of our lives in the present.

While we are pursuing our soul's restoration in the present, bringing old baggage along is not suitable. Self's insecurity relapses on the shame of the past and the future's apprehension. When Jesus is the Lord of our past, unwrapping the possibilities of the present settles our future with an expectancy of good things.

Faith is not complete without repentance and so is repentance without faith. Repentance is a disconnection from our wounded and painful past. Faith, on the other hand, is our connection with our identity and destiny in Christ.

Repentance comes into play to aid faith's continuation. In the absence of faith, repentance has no substance. On the other hand, repentance outfits faith with authenticity and integrity. Repentance completes faith and faith finalize repentance. Prophet Isaiah said.

> *Let the wicked forsake his way, And the unrighteous man his thoughts; Let him return to the Lord, And He will have mercy on him; And to our God, For He will abundantly pardon.*
>
> *Isaiah 55:7 NKJV*

Our thought processes constitute the framework for our life's direction. Our outlook on life decides what our life would be like. Our way of thinking determines the way we live. We are the way we think.

When we focus on the essential thing, trivial things are out of the way. When we awake in righteousness, we sin not. When we concentrate on the right stuff, we end up enjoying its by-product. Blessings graciously fall in place when we seek to pursue the source instead of the desired result.

God will not require us to cut ourselves off from our thoughts and ways without giving us something superior to replace it. In fact, the word 'return' used on Isaiah 55:7 is the English word for "repentance." Revelation knowledge surgically removes our old thoughts and ways from our unrestored soul.

> *"For My thoughts are not your thoughts, nor are your ways My ways," says the Lord; "For as the heavens are higher than the earth so are My ways higher than your ways, And My thoughts than your thoughts.*
>
> *Isaiah 55:8-9 NKJV*

We traditionally use these passages of scripture from Isaiah 55 to excuse and to justify our human frailties but what these verses of scripture are saying is that His ways and thoughts are superior to ours. Instead of our own, God is asking us to embrace His thoughts and ways.

When in humility we relinquish the claim of self-consciousness in our soul, God's greatness is ours for the taking. However, when we let the sense of entitlements gets in the way of God, we limit our life's assessment only to the human level.

Gauging life's challenges with the conviction of Christ's completed victory is available by way of God's thoughts and ways, and they are all found in the Word of God.

The preoccupations of old stuff are hostile for the future prospect; they can throw our focus off. Nevertheless, when we allow a set of eyes that is higher than ours; we see and handle things differently because the elevated platform of the Word of God enables us to regard life beyond our self- absorbed perspective. The truth of God's Word convinces us that our eternal significance only lies on being in the will of God.

The view from the top is far-reaching than what we can appraise life on a human level. We are not up to the challenge when what we only have in our earthly existence is just a natural outlook of life.

When we embrace the fact that we are not capable of living and capturing our destiny outside the help of the Holy Spirit, life is viewed beyond an effort-filled appraisal of self.

As in the absence of His thoughts and ways, we are akin to a barren earth; we only produce nothing. Nonetheless, His thoughts and His ways are like the rain and the snow that provides abundance - a catalyst for growth.

Chapter 3: Breaking Unto Greatness

> *"For as the rain comes down, and the snow from heaven, and do not return there, But water the earth, and make it bring forth and bud, That it may give seed to the sower And bread to the eater, So shall My word be that goes forth from My mouth; It shall not return to Me void, But it shall accomplish what I please, And it shall prosper in the thing for which I sent it.*
>
> *Isaiah 55:10-11 NKJV*

The Spirit's spoken Word discloses God's thoughts and ways. Once perceived and believed in, it will accomplish and prosper the purpose to which God spoke it. Jesus said, "… he who has ears to hear, let him hear what the Spirit of God is saying."

The spiritual connection is one thing but validating the said connection with our hearing ears and our seeing eyes is another. It is us who decide that our hearing ears hear, and our seeing eyes see. To hear Him speak confirms our relationship with Him. On the other hand, obeying what we have heard from Him unveils His greatness over us.

A conviction that is engaged in action separates passion that seeks completion from just an existence of motion. Engaging with our passion and conviction comes easy when we know that our decision is a result of God's revelation. God is on the giving end, and we are on the receiving, He is always speaking to us more than we know it ourselves. However, when we prefer to cater for things that ease our pain and soothes our self-centered life, our focus becomes blurred, and our hearing becomes dull because we are taking God out of the picture.

Jesus said, "…If therefore the light that is in you is darkness, how great is that darkness!" When the revelation of the Word of God is not the basis of our life's pursuit, and we persist regardless; we are telling God, "My seeing eyes are unwilling to see the truth as it is." This rebellion is worse than unbeliever's ignorance. It is nothing but a blind seeing eye.

CHAPTER FOUR
Breakthrough is Decisive
Dare to crossover unto the magnitude of your destiny

Breakthrough Impacts Your World

Years ago, I watched a 1998 film Pleasantville. The theme of the movie is about breakthrough, but I reject the lifestyle of immorality that it suggests.

Pleasantville is a story about two teenage siblings who were mystically sucked into the black hole of a 1950 black and white fictional TV program – Pleasantville, a suburban that depicts a society of status quo, colorless, living in the box, and predictable existence.

The humanly colorful life of these siblings broke out into this monotonous and stagnated grayscale town. From the inside out, these sparkling duo manifests the true colors of their identity and their vibrant glow of non-conformity provoked, impacted, and transformed the suburban's biased and delusional perception of reality.

The whole community ultimately discovered that outside their stiff, lifeless, and stale regimen, life with enriched potentials is available out there on the other side. The siblings made a significant difference of crossing over this tedious society into a world filled with living colors.

As always, there is an antagonist who wants to hinder conversion of life for the better, yet the siblings breaking through of Pleasantville unto the colorful life was unstoppable.[32]

The restriction causes by a life carried out in a perpetual familiar routine is exasperating. It is more of the same every day - a repetitive lifestyle that excludes life's distinctiveness.

Our life's definition is beyond what we can sweat it out on our own. Compensating for our dehydrated religion will ultimately burn us out. Thank God, He has given us a new creation spirit which is dynamic through the potency of God's unconditional forgiveness and acceptance.

Getting dominated again with things that are irrelevant to our destiny are pointless to the essence of our identity in Christ. Eradicating things that the Lord Jesus has already destroyed is not only a purposeless rhetoric, but it is also a life of open-ended dissatisfaction. Adhering to Christ's completed work always causes us to be on top of our game because life starts from the reality of what everything Christ has redeemed us for.

On every front, the religious works of man fails in comparison with the divine enablement of the grace of God. The revelation of His goodness gives us the conviction of turning our back from the world and march forward towards on what the Lord has called us for. Knowing that God's forgiveness is more of redemption than condemnation, helps us understand how to live life out of His goodness. We are loved by Him regardless of what and where we have been. The Lord is our sustainer, He is not our accuser.

God's plan of completing our soul's destiny goes on regardless of what stands our way. As we come to the full understanding that Christ alone is the life that can provide spiritual breakthrough for our soul; consequently, the whole array of Heaven's actual color is dawning on our earthly existence.

Mediocrity: The Enemy of Breakthrough

In his capacity, as United States Commissioner of Patents from 1898 until 1901, Charles Holland Duell allegedly stated his infamous claim; "Everything that can be invented has been invented."[33]

On the other hand, it is hard to conceive what life could have been if we didn't advance technologically. Compares to our present society's modern comfort, 1800's is inconceivable; their living environment was stinky, tedious, and backward.

Thanks to the progressive thinkers who did not let down their creative juice nor allowed themselves to be hindered by their current narrow-minded institutions; they have taken us to the ease of innovative living. Pioneers made hard life easier for all of us! We can all agree that by a long shot, pioneers blazed the trails for others to go through.

There are things in life that are not meant to let go, and mediocrity is not one of them. Mediocrity is a mental attitude that restricts us from getting out of monotonous living unto the exceptional existence.

Mediocrity Defined

The word "mediocre" comes from the Latin compound word "mediocris." "Medius" means middle and "ocris" means rugged mountain.[34] The complete description of the word "mediocre" is, "in half about the rough mountain." Mediocrity is stranded halfway of its goal due to its indulgence to predictability.

Average life despises the unknown. Moving beyond expectation is daunting to a typical person. Going further is always intimidating to a man who surrendered his dream to a usual life.

When the goal of reaching the summit serves as a firm conviction, seeking significance outside our limitation is a worthy passion.

What awaits us at the peak offers us a grand scale perspective for life. Status quo keeps our soul typical, and it hinders us from perceiving Christ's gift of greatness.

Every time we mention a mediocre disposition, cowardice comes to mind. This should not be, because every man that came into this world gets here on earth with the attached purpose in his life.

Since Christ has already redeemed us with His blood, soaring to greater heights is one of our spiritual inheritance. Navigating life beyond the familiar is a burden that is easy and feasible since God has qualified us in Christ to participate with the inheritance of the saints in the light.

What Causes Mediocrity?

Life of mediocrity happens when a man finds gratification in a life that is devoid of purpose and allow himself to be restricted with meager life. Undoubtedly, his fear of responsibility and evasiveness to accountability restrain him from stepping up to the cutting edge.

Instead of breaking new grounds for prospects of graceful expressions, mediocrity detains a man within the confines of non-essentials.

Man reduces himself to a maintenance worker when he abandons himself to be captivated with predictable regimens. On the other hand, a pacesetter is full of curiosity in how he can go about creating something unique to his identity.

Filling in a gift outside your calling inevitably ends up into a mundane life regardless if you disguise your existence in a seemingly fruitful activity. Ambition will reach completion if it falls into the category of true vocation but expecting an impressive result from a façade of a self-glamorous rank will not come to ripening season.

We should never seek position outside God's calling; it is irresponsible, and it is a character that is void of principle, it not only wastes our time and resources but also of others.

Mediocrity Stinks

When Joshua, my oldest son was still a toddler, he drags his security pillow wherever he goes; they were inseparable. He was not only emotionally attached to it, but that pillow's stench defines his blissful sensation. Nevertheless, when he advanced in age and carrying such pillow looks unbecoming of his age; my wife and I did something drastic to break his object of security to something relational.

In perspective, technology is a tool, and it should not be a trap and a pacifier. Undisciplined pastime with our current comfort zones maybe technically cozy, but it can be potentially costly. Left alone with this out of control "selfie" state of mind, our sensitivity to divine essentials will surely diminish and the next thing you know, opportunities slips between our grips.

We must not allow technology to dehumanize us and cause us to lose touch with each other on a personal level. We must break off from this spirit of indifference.

As our current worldly atmosphere increases its layers of evil, so is the accelerations of His grace becomes more apparent to those who pray and watch in the Spirit. We are currently shifting in seasons of God's momentous awakening.

Life can happen faster than the stride of our coming in. We can expect results of an unlikely stipulation when we are ill-equipped to a given challenge. However, discernment will cause us to see the difference.

Mediocrity Blinds

Mundanity in mentality blocks our focus from perceiving our spiritual capacity to carry out our God given identity. We execute what we see ourselves doing and we set life's limits based on how farther we can imagine.

To extremely venture into our life's calling, pulling down the stronghold of mediocrity that illegally squatting in our minds is not an option, but it is a radical path that our faith must take on.

A mind filled with self-reproach is uneasy and prone to repeat what they initially made them guilty in the first place. Sense of condemnation scrambles our focus into self-denunciation.

Maybe you were saying, "this could have been my life if I had not made these wrong choices in the past." The contemplation of; "why to bother, things are hard to come by anyways" blurs one's perception to carry on.

When we explore our God-given possibilities outside our little self-absorbed tendencies, we turned out to be what the Holy Spirit is continually calling our soul out to become.

When we keep on tapping how God perceive things, then we can crack the impossible and able to offer the world of something that they are missing out.

Let us dare to see the magnitude of our destiny in Christ. Our finality is not what and who we are in our soul currently.

Mediocrity Procrastinates

Procrastination is a pacifier in which an average man suck on. Life lived outside its defined purpose procrastinates by trying to live here, there, and everywhere.

Confusion is a repercussion of losing our bearings as our existence ticks its countdown. "Potato couching" as well as "unnecessary" extra-curricular activities cannot fix nor able to dodge the outcome that mediocrity set in motion, it rather speed up the deterioration.

A timely opportunity slips away in between our fingers when we let the spirit of mediocrity creeps in from behind us and shove us to abandon ourselves to status quo.

One may presume that he is only suspending his allotted time, thinking that he is just chilling out for the time being, and he will reconvene himself when everything is conducive to his euphoric zone. The truth is, he is depriving his soul an opportunity to become.[35]

Delaying our soul's spirituality means getting in the way of Heaven to touch our earthly existence. It was purpose defeating scheme when after we were given this life in Christ, then we are not doing anything to cultivate it.

Resting in the Lord does not mean disengagement from doing the will of God; it means actively participating with all the things that Christ has achieved for us on the cross and His resurrection.

Receiving the revelation of what and why God recreated our spirit in Christ conveys wisdom on how we can engage our spiritual identity in these final hours. When the narrative of our inheritance in Christ's is defined, we can then operate our spiritual position in Christ. We set in motion what we passionately believe in.

Jesus said, "…the night is coming, and no one can work."[36] We are not certain when will the darkness' domino effect flips its final piece. Therefore, while there is an opportunity to plug in with our God-given purpose, seizing our moments with God is crucial.

The time is coming when mediocrity will dull the hearts of men, for misperception will obscure their sense of discernment. Mediocrity can weaken our sensitivity to spot the right ground in staging our Spirit-given commission. While it is still called "Today," our mandate is to enforce the will of God.

The light (or the revelation) is a must for us to demonstrate who God is. Without the revelation of the Spirit, we have nothing to offer. Meaning, while we can still go into all the world, let us go and proclaim the Kingdom of God.

If we ever missed this God's divine mandate because we indulge ourselves with our comfort zones, then the world that we neglected to reach out for Jesus will someday will potentially come against us in fury.

Mediocrity Compromises

It is compromisingly easy to drift along with the world's contemporary tide. On the contrary, going against the worldly stream is an ongoing head-on collision that goes against our inward conviction. When we throw in the towel to life's challenges, then we believe that there are no more remaining places for us to explore because our worldly desperation seems to exhaust it all.

Our life in Christ goes beyond the measure of a mediocre mind. Making a difference in our God-given sphere of influence means the breaking of the neutral ground. Shattering mediocrity leads to forward momentum. However, yielding to mediocrity reduces us to wallow ourselves in business as usual.

Nonetheless, living life in familiar existence will not cause our life's purpose to cease to exist, for the Father's stubborn love will not just give us up that easy. He will wait for us to get around on realizing of who we are in Christ.

We all need God to put His wonders on our typicality. In Christ, we can stand our ground beyond the cutting edge and by His grace change the worldly worst unto His paramount best.

When we walk away from the leadership of the Holy Spirit, His creative processes within us is on a standstill. In other words, we let mediocrity compromise our conviction.

The Spirit of God always lead us into the life that champions growth and renewal. The restoration of our soul is a footprint of spiritual headways. Manifestations of victory come through the process of our soul's spiritual breakthrough.

Our lives exceptionally stand out when by the Spirit of God, we breathe the life Jesus from the inside out. Now, the responsibility to tend and develop this world is resting on the shoulders of those who are in Christ.[37]

In Christ, we can definitively rule this world instead of being at the mercy of its elements. Earth and its elements are our servants and not the other way around.

Mediocrity is a Choice

A man becomes a class of second-rate as he allows himself to be. Status quo is a choice. Using our will to engage the intention of God for our lives is a disposition that goes well with our destiny.

Dying to self-conscious soul is not a termination of will, rather it is employing of our will to will the will of God.

Life carried out outside its divine intention is a life irrelatively lived. Mind you, this is the root of all forms of discontentment.

Mediocrity takes away our freedom to explore on things that we are destined to manifests in Christ.

Mediocrity imprisons us within the restriction of typicality. Our soul needs serious spiritual deliverance from such pessimistic habit.

This limiting box of usual life is meant to be broken and dismantled by the revelation of Christ. The spiritual breakthrough of our soul is critical in breaching this hardened attitude of the unrenewed mind.

Breakthrough is Significant

Breakthrough is decisive. It has a sphere of influence on where it can progressively take us into the future. Every spiritual breakthrough of the soul is a moment of renewal with God. It allows us to experience the best part of life that we have not had the practical proficiency before.

Our soul progressively advances to the newness of our spiritual transformation as we steadily catch the new wave of the Holy Spirit, such faith-walk fine-tunes our minds, emotion, and will.

In perspective, what transition us to the next steppingstone is our personal encounter with God; such breakthrough defines our specified season of faith. God's phenomenon is lived through when we learn to stretch our faith amid circumstances.

When our soul spiritually breakthrough, the word challenging is no longer coined as negative, but something that perks our interest.

Embarking outside our human limitations grants us the opportunity to get acquainted with God's abilities. We need God's revelation to understand His mind.

Counter Steer Your Way to Breakthrough

Driving in the polar region is exhilarating. Iced roads are not only slippery, but such road conditions push your nerves to the limit even if you are driving a four-wheel drive vehicle. With years of experience, Alaskans learned to drive through the icy roads when sliding.

They are enjoying the ride as they counter steer their way through the icy roads. Polar drivers recognized that once you abruptly step on the brake, you will be at the mercy of gravity; meaning, you can either ended into a ditch or cause an accident to yourself and others.

Insults will always come from people with little minds, who think they are the ones that has the final say. Do not get intimidated and be at the mercy of their typical mindset. Counter steer your way on these slippery roads, turn the tide and pursue God's destiny sensitive elements for your life.

As you realize that Jesus is the greater One who indwells you, manifestations of greatness is what awaits you. Settling at the cruelty of others is not your appointed doom. You do not belong on the ditches of life or anything that can jam your potentials to a complete halt.

You are God's own man, and you are meant to dance to the tune of His grace allocated to your unique calling. You are preordained to live and do the good works that God predisposed in your recreated spirit. Focus on the image that God has in mind for your soul's spiritual progress.

Disregard the disturbance and interruption from Sanballats and Tobiahs in your life.[38] It is ironic, but we always hear criticism from people who does nothing in everything. Yes, by mounting up our conviction into the open, we inevitably attract the opposition. Welcome to the Club!

When we solely operating our lives by the natural senses, we are predisposed to the angst of life. When our souls are overwhelmed with stress, the rest's condition of our spirit, is not in charge. We could care less about people natural outlook of us when we are operating in His revelation, for we know we have the audience of the One.

Breakthrough Does Not Step on the Brake

The main causes of high volume of traffic condition in Southern California highways are its bottleneck areas. They were not designed to accommodate future population explosions and increase volumes of transportation.

This situation led to an awful commuting concern; the traffic stalled Southern Californians consumes more fuel energy per capita than all their combined regular commuting. What a waste!

Leaving room for advancement decides more breathing room for growth. When we assume that our today's comfort cannot be our future discomfort, then there is no leeway for improvement.

When we opted to be one hit Jack for our soul's transformation, our influence for progress will not go on. Our soul's transformation is an on-going lifestyle; it is never meant to be a hype!

Faith continually advances. Breakthrough keeps on breaking life's restrictions and paves the way to subsequent waves of breakthroughs. It sets up a platform upon thereafter.

Skipping any upcoming stages and concluding the current breakthrough as final is unacceptable. From beginning to the end, every spiritual leaping forward is a steppingstone to the next level until we reach the fullness of our destiny in Christ.

God's momentum never dies down. Growth cannot be a substantial growth without subsequent growth. Success cannot be called success without succeeding successes. Breakthrough cannot be a breakthrough without consequent breakthroughs.

Our life in Christ is a series of breakthroughs. We go from one level of glory unto an ever-increasing level of glory. The reason why the worship of God in heaven never ends, it is because God eternally emanates a divine revelation of Himself.

A constant walk with God is a result of the relentless revelation of His glory. An ongoing personal revelation of God's glory proceeds to a steady expression of growth.

Enoch had 300 years' testimony of walking with God, and during those times, he pleased God as he scaled up through stairway of faith. Daily as he ascended to the succeeding doorways of faith, each completion led him to another path and on and on.

Until the time when it is dawning at the 300th years, his faith reached the point of no return. As his walk consistently pleasing God, his faith outgrew the hold of the imperfect world on him; God broke him through unto the other side.[39]

Our spiritual breakthrough on earth has no stop sign; it will continue to breed an ongoing breakthrough until the heaven rends and finally cracks its complete manifestation on the earth. Until then, we will keep on breaking to breakthrough in Christ. The Eternal Father is continually unveiling His transforming glory through His Spirit and His Word, supplying one revelation towards one firm conviction at a time.

Breakthrough is Record Breaking

Therefore, leaving the discussion of the elementary principles of Christ, let us go on to perfection...

Hebrews 6:1 NKJV

Breakthrough is monumental because it is a history changer. In 1948, the sound barrier was officially broken, and thus ushered us into the jet age, and we now transport things quicker and efficiently.

In olden days, you need an entourage of employees to undertake an executive business trip. Nowadays, all you need is a Wi-Fi connection, and you are setup for real-time video conferencing with the rest of the world. If somehow, we stopped from the comfort zone of our rotary phone, and we did not adapt to succeeding communication technologies, smartphones will not be around today.

Breakthrough fills the gap of limitation and creates momentum for growth. We have never been the same again because of a breakthrough. If growth is not our aspiration, demoralization is on the brink of our horizon.

Breakthrough is a historical signpost. We must leave something to go somewhere. In these last days, God is changing the spiritual game plan, from the rudimentary unto leaping forward of our destiny.[40]

God is priming the church for greatest resurgence of His glory. Today's technology is not an accident. The current global technological awareness is being framed up by God for the next greatest manifestation of Himself that the earth has never seen yet.

Where sin advances, the grace of God proliferates even more. The move of God thrives despite current changes. Game plans may change because of today's intensity of evil. However, Jesus is always the same yesterday, today and forever. Jesus the Truth is relative for all generation.

We customized with the seasons of change but not to the point of compromising the truth. We cannot institutionalize the truth, but we can always bring the truth to our contemporary world. We cannot disregard the basics; we grow heights on basic foundations.

In 2012, while driving in the city of Anchorage, Alaska, I had this spontaneous flash of inward revelation that; "God will hold us responsible if we as the Church of Christ will not take advantage of our current technology for the rapid propagation of the Gospel." Can we have a cassette tape approach in a 5G world?

As the Body of Christ, we should adapt to available technologies of the days. With these entire technological breakthroughs, God has something in mind that we need to grasp.

There is no gear to crank in neutrality. We either do forward shifting or reversing. Either downhill or uphill stance, gravity affects our location when our gear is in neutral position.

A person who positions himself on nothing will never come to the point of growing. Let us recognize this provision for acceleration and do something about it.

In medieval times, people were afraid of navigating the seven seas, because the established mindset at that time says that the world is flat. During such era, ocean exploration will not go further the unknown because of the fear of plummeting at the edge of the earth.

The best man to pioneer a decisive breakthrough is the person who will find ways to connect the current condition with a permanent solution. At times, it will only take one dedicated man for revival to break out.

Columbus is the man! He did not fear the unknown nor regarded the persecution from the established religious and educational institution of the day; he broke through from their false belief and proved their doctrinal standing as false.

After his discovery that the earth is round, Columbus opened the channel for earth's various explorations. Have you ever wondered why despite the fact, there are still flat earthers?

When spiritual breakthrough happens, there is a shifting that transpired in the mindset of the Body of Christ; we unlearn the old doctrines that never works, and we welcome the fresh revelation of the Word.

For years, we have been taught to make disciples of an individual in Christ. People wrote books about it and launched conventions and seminars for just about personal discipleship; they are essential but the mandate we receive from Christ is,

> *"Go therefore and make **disciples of all nations**, baptizing them in the name of the Father, and of the Son, and of the Holy Spirit, teaching them to observe all things that I have commanded you…"*
>
> *Matthew 28:19-20 NKJV*

Jesus has a bigger picture in heart than what we currently specialized on. God's mandate for us is to take over the world under His authority and dominion. God has not changed His mind yet since He told Adam to rule the earth and have authority over it.

Nowadays, it seems that the earth and earthly calamities are taking over, and humans are at their mercy. In God's economy, the divine order is always the other way around.

The real spiritual breakthrough will shift our mindset to see the world based on God's perspective and not on the religious box that we strain ourselves to believe.

Spiritual breakthrough is a forward shifting of nation's mindset, and moral collapse is a nation on a spiral spiritual breakdown. Today's current revival of the Holy Spirit sets the Body of Christ up in a strategic position for global domination.

CHAPTER FIVE
The Making of a Breakthrough
Breakthrough happens in life's in-between

God's Mercy: The Basis of Life's Continuity

> *22 Through the Lord's mercies we are not consumed, Because His compassions fail not. 23 They are new every morning; Great is Your faithfulness. 24 "The Lord is my portion," says my soul, "Therefore I hope in Him!*
>
> *Lamentation 3:22-24 NKJV*

When each morning we find ourselves breathing and able to navigate our senses around, this is a daily token of God's love where in a way He is reminding us; "I believe that what I invested within you will make its way to its fullest expression, and you can finish the race of faith that I set before you." If this is not so, we are no longer here by now. Right? Indeed!

The Lord knows that His love never fails. Let us come to imagine how long He has been dealing with us, but He never even entertain a thought of giving us up. God's enduring mercy consistently stretches a hedge of protection around us.

God is ever hopeful that in our earthly lifespan, we can decisively come to the full realization of our soul's divine destiny. The entirety of humanity's hope towards Him pale in comparison with what God is hoping for you and me.

It is incredible to realize that we are still around despite of everything that we have been through. His hope preserves us; thus, His grace is blowing our mind in ways beyond what we can reason among ourselves.

It is obvious that we savor the renewal of His loving kindness every time the sun rises and the rain pours. Has it ever occurred to you that every day is a brand-new day? Each day respectively unpacks new expectation of good things.

Jesus said, "God the Father makes the sun rise on the evil and the good and sends rain both to the just and to the wicked."[41] Amidst life's challenges, God's mercy allows us to continue.

If we can only fully grasp the way God the Father sees us in Christ, no one can stop us from manifesting the Kingdom of God in words and in power. He has given us His Life, His Spirit, His Word, His Mind, His Wisdom, and His Righteousness.

All that we are and have in Christ are ours because we are His. He knows that with everything that He invested within our recreated spirit, we are equipped to break through in every given challenge that will come along our way.

What Happened in Between?

Standing where we currently at unto the expression of our next season of faith is the challenging part of our spiritual journey. However, at the dawn of the finishing touches of our crossing over, it is effortless.

There is no opportunity to rest our confidence on His good Word if we are living in a perfect world. Amidst obstacles and complications though, the conviction of Jesus' resurrection life within us is our unshakable courage that enable us to break through the pressing exertion of adversity.

> *I do not pray that you should take them out of the world but that you should keep them from the evil one. They are not of the world, just as I am not of the world. Sanctify them by your truth. Your Word is truth.*
>
> John 17:15-17 NKJV

'Don't Take Them Out of this World'

Earth is the place where our soul can spiritually breakthrough. An earthly challenging event is a turning point where we can make the most of our divine opportunity. In heaven, there is no more spiritual leaping forward, because such is the place where we will celebrate our ultimate victory throughout eternity.

Our earthly existence in Christ is a lifestyle that journeys from faith to faith. What initiates the pursuit of the will of God in our lives is the faith (rhema) that we initially heard from the Spirit of God, and what brings us closer to our soul's fullest potential is the faith (rhema) that consummated into the completion of our assignment of the season.

Often, what happened in between is rarely mentioned. What has become the Church's tunnel vision is the over emphasis of faith's kickoff and faith's outcome.

What determines the continuity of the manifestation of our identity in Christ is not the initial burst of faith or the highlight of faith's outcome, but what decisively happened between the emerging faith and the proceeding faith.

The in-betweens are where our soul spiritually breaks through and display God's glory and goodness. Notice how the scripture says it; "...from faith TO faith." Growth is the process of God's Kingdom.

During life's procedures, practical expressions of spirituality become apparent when we engage our faith on, because in-between the culmination of our heavenly call and our earthly existence, are opportunities to manifest our spiritual connection with our Heavenly Father. In other words, the breakthrough of God's divine momentums is crank up in between faith episodes of our lives.

What creatively and decisively demonstrated amidst the commencement of faith and its consummation is the highlight of the outcome of the Holy Spirit's direction. It is a decisive focal point towards revealing the invisible Christ's cosmos to the world of chaos.

It is during this time that while we are having done all to stand, by His grace our faith is kept standing still until the other side is broken through.

What enlarges our soul's capacity to receive and increases our handle for greater things is the outcome that we get from Lord's dealing amidst life's procedure.

Life's inevitabilities are guaranteed to happen in this imperfect world where we live. Often, we complicate our appointed times and seasons when we try to help God out. When the going gets tough, the only sensible thing that we can do is to take God at His Word.

Once the Lord's mind is understood towards life challenges, we do not see challenging stuff as nuisances anymore, but we view it as a project from God that we are equipped to complete.

Problems are life's prospects poses the wrong way up. Our God's endowed creativity is His method of madness where we skillfully read and exploit such life's complications and turned it the right way up.

Life challenges are opportunities for us to live our faith from the inside out. There is no way for us to work out what God has worked inside of us if there are no opportunities to manifest it. Living in the spirit is walking our existence by the conviction of the Word of God amidst circumstantial complications. Such is a faith walk and not a sight ruled life's inclination.

For spiritual growth, Jesus signed us up where divine and human dynamics are plenty to go around. Truly, part of God's plan is our current earthly existence where opportunities crucial to our life's faith episodes are not lacking. This world is a place where we further the Lord's divine intention on this earth. We thrive as the Lord stretches our soul on earth.

Often, we waste too much time looking for advancement opportunities elsewhere when all the while; they are all in and around us. Look all around, opportunities are everywhere. In fact, you can see that opportunity every time you face that mirror. Yes! You! You are a piece of work! You are indeed an opportunity for growth! Or maybe your break for growth is your spouse who stands right next to you, or possibly the people who you rub shoulders every day.

These mentioned opportunities are the very crosses in which the Holy Spirit exposes our undealt self-restricting personas that are illegally residing in our soul. We cannot be a manifestation of living soul for God on earth until His glory saturates our mind, emotion, and will. Here on this planet, the endless growth opportunities are immensely way beyond the roof. Neither whichever way we turn nor wherever we choose to be, adversities are inevitably plenty. In life, there are no shortages of challenges.

Evading them is an absurdity that accomplishes nothing. However, through the Holy Spirit's anointing and revelation, life's true worth shines when problems are turned the other way around. When Jesus prayed; "I do not pray that you should take them out of the world," He knew what He was exactly praying over.

A fulfilled divine destiny is a result of God at work with a man who is sold out with His plan. Doing God's will propel us to our soul's divine destiny. As we are trekking our earthly spiritual journey, bubbling up our identity in Christ launches us out into our divine purposes.

The signpost of genuine spiritual commitment is a life consistent with all that we claimed we believe. God the Father sent Jesus His Son to reveal to us His will. Jesus is the Straight and Narrow Way, the Truth that liberated us from darkness, and He is our Life with the Father. So, until we receive the revelation and start believing all that Christ has come into this world for, we will not be able to do the work of God on earth. The Gospel according to John says,

> *Then they said to Him, "What shall we do, that we may work the works of God," Jesus answered and said to them, "This is the work of God that you believe in Him whom He sent."*
>
> *John 6:28-29 NKJV*

'Sanctify Them in Your Truth'

While we are here on earth, God's truth has a way of consistently setting our soul apart as we draw our significance from our heavenly citizenship. Therefore, outside the reality of God's Word, life in this world is enslaving.

On the other hand, what unwraps God's plan with confirmation of freedom is our agreement with God's revealed truth. Standing in harmony with His Word decides a liberated and prosperous soul that exemplifies the Kingdom's inheritance.[42]

The truth defines man for divine service; it sanctifies his soul from all incapacitating lies and deceptions. Admiring the truth is one thing but grasping its redemptive power is another. To those who came to its realization through the revelation of the Spirit of God, the truth is meant to convey freedom.

When you are free, you can unleash everything the Lord has given in your life. The Holy Spirit will not be called as the Spirit of Truth for nothing.

What is keeping the Holy Spirit from emanating the glory of God in our earthly existence, is the condition of our soul. When we let, the truth takes the ownership of our soul's persona; we trigger the divine releases of heaven every time we connect with God in the spirit. We manifest an out of this world phenomenon when the revelation of the truth links us up with the Spirit of God.

Indeed, our divine connection with God is based on "in spirit and truth." IN SPIRIT, because subjectively, our relationship with the Father revolves on the life that He already set us up with in Christ. IN TRUTH, because our soul must objectively focus on responding to the reality of Jesus' cross and His resurrection.

Every time we flow in the Spirit revealed truth, the reality of our divine connection manifests on earth in a greater way. When the truth-based spiritual pursuit goes down to our nitty-gritty, it triggers divine activity to come about in our faith community.

You see, God the Father by the Holy Spirit gave us spiritual ears which are on the same playing field with Him. We can hear God's voice. However, we may time and again heard what the Holy Spirit is saying, but it is still up to us to engage ourselves on what God has personally told us.[43]

The Spirit's conviction of Christ Lordship is near our hearts and our mouth, and yet it is still our choice to let Him be the Lord. When we keep on refusing to let our hearing ears listen to what the Holy Spirit is revealing and prompting, we are in effect choosing our hearts to become callous to His direction.

Jesus said, "from the innermost being of every believer, shall rivers of living water flows." There is nothing more satisfying than experiencing our place becomes a temporarily part of His realm where He Himself shows up. The Bible says,

> For the eyes of the Lord run to and fro throughout the whole earth, to show Himself strong on behalf of those whose heart is loyal to Him...
>
> 2 Chronicles 16:9 NKJV

The Hebrew word for the word 'loyal' in the abovementioned scripture is "shalem." It means "to be at peace," or "to be in agreement."[44] God is constantly watchful of souls that are entirely in agreement with His Truth (which is Jesus and all that He accomplished in His cross and His resurrection).

Once the Lord affirms such soul's persona, then God the Father has a man in whom He can manifest His glory to this world. Christ's liberating truth, separates, and sanctions our soul for God's revival when we become willing to stand unprotected from any self-entitlement.

God Defines a Man

By using his all-time favorite "yes, I know" comeback line, a self-proclaimed genius son often smashes his dad's relentless and annoying recaps.

Shortly thereafter, reality check came knocking on his face when this Einstein had a head-on collision with one significant financial responsibility.

The father gladly jumped into his son's case and greeted him; "come on in my boy, welcome to the land of the living!" As the father opened the door of practicality to his inexperienced child so to speak, he whispered into his son's ear as he passes by; "Now, I surely know, you know!"

As a guiding principle, the wise should not be at the mercy of the presumptuous one. Without a doubt, presuming from just a notion will make a fool out of you when the whole truth comes into view.

Assuming words that we claimed as "the final say so" are deemed irreversible when in an awkward moment such claim proves to be a summation of a false impression. The only way out of this self-prophetical embarrassment is the admission of the mistake done.

Either Jesus defines the man, or he is characterized by his reluctance. If we cannot admit that we are wrong, then God's truth cannot release us from the falsehood of our pride.

Truth eludes us until we experientially come across with it. Authenticity can only be best served on the table of experience and not on the menu of human intelligence.

When our knowledge practically displays our true being in Christ, circumstances is lived out as harnessed life's prospects.

The truth is what other persuasions cannot convey; human supposition only communicates idealism and reasoning. God's intervention amidst the launching and the culmination of life's faith episodes is our life's God-given defining moment.

Life skills turn out for good when we experience what we know. We best educate ourselves by the knowledge that we come to encounter; such realism of life carries more weight for they are heat-treated, and pressure processed in the grind.

Knowledge comes about by learning, while wisdom comes to light by living and experiencing its outcome. If the Master learned and experienced results of His obedience, then can we be greater than Jesus - our Master?[45]

Earthly Relevance of Heaven's Reality

By a long shot, life resonated in experience is quickly absorbed and understood. Indeed, we can only impart the thing that is already a part of us. Conveying a seized divine moment is a stimulating testimony, for it carries more weight than mere human knowledge.

Sharing an encounter with God transmits an anointing of victory. Besides, one of God's weapon that incapacitates the influence of the enemy is the testimony of God in our lives.[46]

Information contributes knowledge, but verifications passes on spiritual inspiration. What deeply touches and soothes people's hearts is the sharing of the tasted goodness of God. In Christian service, our divine encounter with God sharpens our spiritual sword more perceptive than any theological propensity.

Nobody can convince us to go back and re-polishes the chain of bondages that we were once shackled once we experienced our true spiritual freedom.

In the light of this view, John the Beloved sets spiritual experience as the demarcated lines between spiritual fathers, spiritual young man, and spiritual children.[47] On the other hand, knowledge and sound theology are not that all irrelevant, they're useful for checking and balancing every spiritual revelation that we'll bump into along the way.

Common sense and logical deductions have their proper place in our earthly life, but they can never take the prime position of God's spiritual revelation.

Co-Laboring with God

There are two spiritual experiences that are beyond the ability of man: first, is the regeneration of our spirit in the Kingdom of God; secondly, is the redemption of our mortal bodies at the coming of Christ.

These spiritual episodes are exclusively God's doing, and they are beyond man's capacity to perform. New birth is instantaneous. Also, at Christ's appearing, immortality will swallow up our mortal bodies in the twinkling of an eye.

In contrast, our soul's transformation happens within our earthly existence, and it occurs within the vicinity of time and space. Our mind gradually transfigured from glory to glory, from faith to faith, and from grace upon grace.

It is a course of progression that falls under the category of time (intervals) and space (leading in between) processes. When a man engaged his faith with the revealed will of God, the Holy Spirit helps him to carry it out, this results to his soul's spiritual growth continuity.

Our soul is the arena where God's truth is constantly being dared and confronted by the treachery of the enemy; it is an ongoing clash for spiritual supremacy.

Carnality ridden soul is a door for corruption, but a transformed soul surges the flow of eternal life and peace (God's divine order).

Our soul is a go-between our spirit and our body, it is an intermediary between God's supernatural realm and our natural world. Therefore, our soul's restoration means that our soul is being personalized to the level of our born-again spirit.

Our soul is a doorway where God manifest His heaven on earth. The manifestation of God's realm on our earthly existence transpires when our soul breaks through spiritually.

When we break out from "all things" and encountered the truth of "above all things," then our soul becomes an active door where heaven's divine health and prosperity streams.[48]

Spiritual Encounter Spills over the Glory of God

Do you have any idea who and what awaits your soul's spiritual breakthrough? What God may want to do with you after your soul have spiritually broken through? God anointed you with gifts and calling for certain people; you have a divine privilege and responsibility of opening doors for them.

Our experience of His glory blazes the trail of God's realm for those who are following us. Yes, our continual divine encounter with God builds a steady pathway for us and others to walk through. By seizing our moments with God, spiritual legacy is passed on. Knowing, understanding, believing, and experiencing God are elements of our sound spiritual stewardship.

The catalysts for the move of God to transpire is Christ – the Head - directing the movement, and the Church – the Body - allowing the experience flow of the movement. The creations were all made for us, and we were created solely for God. We complete the whole creation when God completes our soul. The whole creations are waiting for us to manifest who we are in Christ.[49] Heaven can flow through when the portal is cracked wide open.

We Become Moldable

The opportunity of molding our soul into the image of Christ transpires in between the inception and the completion of a faith's episode in our lives. Jesus said, "follow me, and I will make you…"[50]

Chapter 5: The Making of a Breakthrough

Engaging our faith to everything that Jesus represented, launches our soul towards God's divine intention; that is, we (the real us – our recreated spirit) possessing the promise land of our minds.

Our receptivity with the reality of Christ's redemption is fundamental to our soul's spiritual breakthrough. So, when we decide to stick with what the Lord has achieved for us through His cross and resurrection, Jesus then commences on shaping our soul in the same wavelength with His Spirit.

The very heart of God is not just to save us from hell but that our soul comes to the full measure of Christ's stature. Jesus is the template of the Kingdom of the New Creation – a Man full of the Holy Ghost and power, a Son who is full of grace and truth.

Understanding the heartbeat of God facilitates a faith that sees through the eyes of Christ and handle things in life through His hands. When we agree with God's plan, we are aligning our soul to our God's divine purpose which He already established within our new creation spirit.

Before we got born again, every fabric of our being was driven with fear. Since we are now in Christ, acting upon what we believe is our spiritual directive. Initially, we were saved by grace through faith. Now, through faith in His grace, we outflow our Christ-given salvation. Such life is beyond the grasp of human fear-based effort, and such is the liberty we have been given in Christ where through faith, God's glory is being released through us.

When there is revelation of God's will, there is understanding of His way. Refusing to acknowledge and understand His will is costly, perplexing, tedious and tiresome. However, when God's will become the source of our disposition, fruit yielding becomes normal spirituality.

When we engage our faith under the guidance of the Holy Ghost, the significance of God's Kingdom is all that we outflow. When the revelation of Christ is received, understood, pursued, and completed, then the Holy Spirit shifts our soul to the next level of understanding our inheritance in Christ. Growing in grace, faith, and glory is maturing in our understanding on who we already are in Christ.

A heart that is characterized by the proclamation of; "with Christ I have everything," leaks out the divine treasure within us to enrich our place of influence. Some doors cannot be opened by any other means except by a soul seized by the glory of God.

At times, directives for our soul's transformation can be trivial, or significant in scale. Nevertheless, to whatever extent it comes our way, what is hanging in the balance is the realization of our soul's spiritual destiny.

Our sensitivity and yielding to God's voice fashions our adaptability with His plan. Reflecting God's glory on a calloused countenance is incomprehensible. The grace of Christ and pride do not go along together, pride and the will of God repel each other.

God resists pride,[51] every time haughtiness miscues the right season. Humility means our will is bendable and adaptable to God's will.

Humility speaks volume because it attracts the inexhaustible grace of the Lord. Humility keeps us from humiliation. Nonetheless, pride's inevitable consequence always surprises a man in his awkward position.

What decides the greatness of the outcome is the depths of our devotion to Christ's revelation. Thus, a character that is defined by Christ's reality amidst adversity is what handle things in life together. To change our soul's consistency from hardened persona onto a character who is willing to learn, the process of breaking our soul's strongholds are essential.

Recurrently, we undergo life's difficulties to put our soul's consistency into the open. However, God is faithful to supply us a way of escape in seasons of testing. God's provision of victory over temptation is received by an ear that is not only able to hear but it also willing to hear. Not everyone that hear the voice of God is willing to heed on what the Spirit is saying.

It is on the putting on of the new man that we're able to put off the old man.[52]   What demolishes soul's carnal inclinations is the likeness of Christ that is being built up in the realm of our soul.

Although Jesus prayed to the Father that we would not be taken out of this world; nonetheless, He sets us apart from the world with the revelation of His Word while we are still on our earthly existence.

We will not be illuminated by darkness; only the Light dispels darkness. Only the Truth sets us free. We cannot say that circumstances purge us spiritually, only the revelation of His Word supplies the faith that sets us apart from the system of this world.

The Proving of Our Will

Amidst the onset and the completion of faith's episode in life, is an occasion where our will is proven. We either follow our will and thus making ourselves our own man or by walking along with His will, we then allow Christ to demonstrate us as His new creation man.

It defeats the purpose of testing when God knows everything. However, when it comes to carrying out His divine eternal purpose, just like His dealing with Abraham, God must prove our will because He leaves it all up to us to engage our faith with His amazing plan. Our will is the hinge on which we carry out God's will or altogether abandon it.

Unless our will conforms to God's will, the earth cannot be one with heaven. God left it all up to the Church - His Body to practically possess the land.

The only thing that God has no influence of and direct control of is our sovereign will. God is extremely unwilling to violate our will. For God to breach man's free moral agency is in total violation of His Word, because He created man after His likeness and in His image. Just like God, man has a sovereign will.

Life's inevitability assaults our inward conviction. Nonetheless, he who walks by faith onto the end will have soul's destiny validation. What secures our spiritual loose ends is the blessing of doing God's will.

When we value the will of God as our own, it pays with an unusual dividend. Once a purpose of God in a specified season ran its course completion, the will of God becomes evident as good, acceptable, and perfect.

An Established Footing

Amidst the commencement and the culmination of life's faith episodes is the opportunity of consolidating our soul's spirituality.

Divinely attached to our life are the prospects of participation with God's divine plan. We highlight the desire to manifest the heart of God in our lives when our heart's sole focus is the will of God.

We radiate our identity in Christ in its truest sense when God's revelation is engaged in faith's affirmation.

Life will not exist exceptionally well outside its attached purpose. There is more to life than just being in the flare of its natural confinement. Our heart beats for something larger than ourselves.

When we are entirely insensitive to what God has in mind for our lives, we are nothing but a blood pumping piece of meat. If what we can only recognize to settle in our lives are its material appeals, then life is ridiculously lost within its physical restriction.

Settling our life with just what we can naturally interact, sets us up unto a shifting foundation. A life based on natural existence alone is unstable. For the lack of the better term, we are easily displaced by the natural turn of events if walking by sight is what only motivates our lives. Nonetheless, we significantly exist when God's divine purpose attached to our life is consistently pursued.

Life is Being, it is not Trying

A life lived outside its attached purpose is an existence that runs in a persistent and wearisome striving.

Existence is a state of being and not a position of exasperating. If you are trying to breathe, this indicates that you have an abnormal physical condition.

Life sustains by the presence of God is a prevailing lifestyle but striving to live life on our own is an existence that cycle in presumption. Compensating for what is lacking is the sole motivation of an apprehensive standpoint, but when we are full of the Holy Ghost, the divine sense of completeness invades our soul.

Therefore, when our divine life statement – we are the righteousness of God in Christ - is understood and received, our faith then is in the resting posture. When we view problems, challenges, and circumstances through the perspective of God's faithfulness, we then just rest on the good Word of the Lord as opposed to trying to squeeze water out of the dry towel.

When we allow our physical senses to impose its urges and let ourselves to get captivated; thus, fleshly complaints will constantly harass our mind, emotion, and will.

Whining is pathetic and worst yet failing on any given time; "I don't think I am doing a harmful thing; I am just nitpicking on life details" as we may interject to say.

Well, anything that does not magnify the works of God pumps up the works of the evil one. Complaining is a communication of pain. It is destructive. It tears down hope, confidence, and even breaks good relationships. Not to mention, creative juice cannot be squeezed out of grouchiness.

Tests and trials are in themselves a spiritual warfare. With just our natural wits alone, we do not have the likelihood of manifesting Christ's victory against any opposition. Knowing where we were coming from and where we are going to, offers us our life's queue. Therefore, coming out from a natural strength to undertake a spiritual journey is an altogether outright failure.

The Holy Spirit continually supplies us with faith that overcomes worldly system. Nonetheless, we will always end up like a puppet being manipulated by the devil through strings of carnal emotions when we try to manage the storms of life based on our natural aptitude.

Natural is natural, spiritual is spiritual. Therefore, striving to be spiritual based on the natural strength is abnormal. To those who walk in the Spirit and not after the flesh, God's way of seeing things is available and accessible. Daily conveyance of our righteousness position in Christ is beyond what our natural senses can gauge. Spirituality is first a position, and when its revelation is engaged in faith, then it operates as a function. The grace of a saved life is only received and operated through faith believing. No more and no less!

God constituted our destiny from the eternity past.[53] What outflow our divine destiny written on the tablet of our hearts, is our present engagement with His will.

Our rendezvous with His will resonates what God envisioned about who we are in Christ. By capturing the revelation of God's divine design that He attributed within our recreated spirits, our identity in Christ is decisively maximized.

Being Built Upon the Rock

> ... On this rock I will build My church, and the gates of Hades shall not prevail against it.
>
> Matthew 16:18 NKJV

It does not take a rocket science to understand that a structural collapse is caused by a weak foundation. So, any persuasion that is not founded on the revelation of the Word of God will always fall apart in difficult times. For sure, a reckless emotion always drives a purposeless mind.

Value emanates from a foundational core. Hence, a character is not a creation of chance. Amid instability, what keeps our hearts and minds in perfect peace is the spoken Word that shines His goodness on us.

It is the revelation of the gospel of Christ that solidifies the disposition of our soul. However, the spoken Word of the Lord carries out its purpose when faith engages it.

The reception and the confession of the revelation that Jesus is the Christ prophetically rendezvous Simon with his destiny. A spiritual revelation is our invisible bridge that crosses over our spiritual conviction unto its fulfillment.

Every time we engage our faith based on the revealed Word of God; the Rock of Christ's anointing epitomizes our divine measured calling in the Body of Christ.

Nothing can be further from the truth to say that; the flow of God's anointing goes along with the revelation of the Word. The gates of hell are defenseless against the revelation of who Christ is.

You cannot be wrong when you do the will of God; because every obedience energized by a revelation has a preordained subsequent divine outcome. All God's promises are yes, and up to the end, we can say, "I agree or Amen!"[54]

God uses His forever-settled Word and the supply of eternal hope of the Holy Spirit, to position us steadfastly. God is not a fickle minded God! No, He is not! Jesus is not a fluctuating foundation either. He is not yes now and no later Lord. God's immutability is His throne's respectability.

The character of God is our strong foundation that undergirds our faith's endeavors and enterprise.[55] His faithfulness is the basis of His glory, dominion, and divinity. The Scriptures says,

> *For we can do nothing against the truth, but for the truth.*
>
> *2 Corinthians 13:8 NKJV*

Despite of all deceptions around us, the truth stands on its own. It cannot be twisted and remain as truth. Truth is not characterized by lies or mixed with truth; a lie does not constitute the truth's consistency either. The truth is pure.

The Word of God is the truth despite human imperfection and bad behavior. Its validity does not depend on our human experience. However, we rely on the Word for our authenticity.

When our stance has its foundation on what Jesus accomplished and completed, nothing can intimidate us. The Gospel is the power of God that manifests Christ's salvation.

Unless what becomes the main thrust of our soul's perception is what Jesus laid His life for, our existence will continuously spin in external religion. The scope of what the cross of Christ did for us is beyond what life as usual can secure.

His substitutionary death is the fullest expression of God's love to mankind. It is redeeming, forgiving, liberating, and sustaining. Enforcing Jesus' settled victory over the war that is waging in the battlefield of our minds is the faith that settles our stability.

Bridging the Gap

When the gap between the faith's commencements and faith's completions is bridged, it results into the access of our next spiritual assignments. In other words, it accommodates continuity.

Truly, our life in Christ are successions of breaking through to freedom, and each freedom we encountered is more liberating than the previous.

The gap that is lacking for the world to witness is the church's participation with God's glory. The essence of eternal life on the inside is the basis of what we can manifest on the outside. External confirmation of life eternal is an essential expression for the world to see Christ through us.

> ...If you continue in my Word, You are my disciples indeed, then you shall know the truth and the truth, will set you free.
>
> John 8:31-32 NKJV

Notice Jesus said, "...if you continue in my Word..." The Lord Jesus didn't say, "...when you continue in my Word...." The word 'IF' is qualifying word and it indicates a stipulation where conditions must be completed first to experience the expected result.

Oppositely, the word 'WHEN' signifies an occasion; it can be opted out or chosen. The word 'IF' signifies a mandate, whereas, 'WHEN' denotes coming into a juncture of doing it.

What Jesus is saying in these verses of scripture is that basis ensures continuity. We were led into an outcome because we engaged ourselves through the process. Experiencing Christ's liberating truth is one thing and continuing in the process of staying in His Word is another.

Resorting to status quo always results to useless exertion of "hyping" things up. In the Kingdom of God, it is not about what you have nor what you do not have, but it is all about Who you know and your divine connection. When our thoughts and ways line up with God's, our hearts are positioned where God's provision flows.

What happened between the launching and the culmination of the episode of faith in our lives cannot be taken too lightly, because it can be a leaping forward of our calling or our downward spiral of our falling.

Breakthrough is an experience of divine truth. Breakthrough is a connection that bridges the gap between the revelation and the manifestation.

When we participate with His will, we strategically position ourselves to receive supplied provision from the Holy Spirit that will fill the gap. The move of God or revival for that matter is brought out when an environment is conducive for the Holy Spirit to flow.[56]

Every believer is a good ground where God's plan can come to fruition. God the Father gave us the grace of His life; it is all up to us to welcome and receive it through faith.

The glorious condition of the Bride is the catalyst that accelerates Christ's Second Coming. The book of Ephesians says, "He will come for a glorious bride." The Bridegroom will never marry an immature church but an immaculate bride of Truth.

The Bride of Christ must come to the point where she can be in a place of agreement with the Holy Spirit, so the two of them can agree and ask; "Come Bridegroom come."

If we keep on living a life based on carnal impulses, and we keep on missing out, and we're not filling in the gap; we, as the now generation Bride of Christ, will not be able to trigger the King's coming.

Our hiccup was and still is that we are passively waits for the second coming of Christ. It is going to take an active participation of Christ's Body to bring back the King. The Word of the Lord says, "Occupy till I come."

We are mandated to complete something with the life that He gave us and then the end will come. Are we occupying what God commanded us in Christ?

The Highlight of Shifting

The season of a spiritual shifting redefines and adjusts our focus and direction.

A spiritual transition is contingent to our growth and maturity in the Kingdom of God, whereas the absence of adaptability reduces us as being ineffective. Yes, we can still do the usual things, but will you be contented when that is all there is to it?

New Covenant proclamation of the Gospel is beyond nominal preaching; it is a demonstration of the power of God. What happen in our life's in-between are opportunities where we can engage our God-given revelation and conviction in the NOW, such faith appointment positions us to our NEXT.

A spiritual transition is ironic. It is an entrée way and a way out at same time. The exit door from the life of familiarity is our entrance to new things of the Spirit.

The new is the exit door of the old. There is no departure from the old without shifting to new things of the Spirit. Our old traditional way around is no match to thwart the tide of current evil times.

Now is the season of fresh winds and new waves of the Spirit. The Holy Spirit is shifting our staging ground from the pulpit of religion unto the manifested presence of God.

In this last days, I believe that the Holy Spirit's global movement of worship in the Body of Christ will usher in the coming of the King of kings and the Lord of lords.

For some, transformation comes with a territory. What makes people hesitate to join the Lord's bandwagon of growth is that God's order always disrupts our long-standing church's tradition. Sitting tight and idolizing our religious' pride and joy is our way of saying; "we are standing in the Lord's way."

The Lord is always ready to shift us to our next spiritual plane. Christ is our solution and the source of our blessings. Therefore, what settles our spiritual transition is our election of following Christ.

Lessons learned means lessons lessened. The understanding of the Truth grows from one level to the next spiritual height. Unless we understand and conquered the test that is specified unto a particular life's season, going through in the same old predicament will be the spinoff of the same pain and aggravation.

When everything routinely revolves around an identical situation - same thing different days, same preoccupation different people; a prospect that inspires hope to the world is rarely find.

If we cannot point to the dot what makes natural and practical life vibrant, then we are all reduced to people who shoot arrows in the dark.

Our capacity to perceive and receive spiritual instructions increases as we align our soul with the will of God; we thus become the Lord's bread that feeds the hungry nations. Well-wisher is one thing, but demonstrators of the Kingdom are what the rest of the creation, the Holy Spirit, and Jesus are groaning in intercession.

God aims for the completion of your destiny than where and who you are at currently. He is more fascinated by what the Holy Ghost can help our soul to become. Yes, God can take a downtrodden and turn him to be His man. He can take you where you are at and bring you to the place where He wants you to be.

God can stretch a life of mediocrity into a life of endless possibilities. God may start you with a simple drop of a spontaneous thought in your spirit, and that inspiration can take you to places way beyond your wildest dreams. Revelation can roll into something greater that blesses humanity if God the One who initiated it, is also the One orchestrating it.

Jesus - Our Point of Reference

A 'point of reference' means a point in space that outlines the initial spot of passage towards a destination. It is a fixed point of position which can be used to refer a starting point towards a designated endpoint. A 'point of reference' is something we use to evaluate, understand, and call out a position or aspects.

A pointless lifespan is a wasted existence. Each path that we take on is an aimless proposition when we purposelessly get on to life's journey. Therefore, venturing to the unknown is beyond what we can naturally survey when a navigational reference is lacking. Unless His plan defines our lives, we will keep trying to exist here, there, and everywhere.

Only the spirituality of faith can tap into the spiritual dimension. A faith walk is a must in experiencing God's realm. Walking by faith is walking through His eyes, His thoughts, His ways, and His love. His Word helps us orient our spiritual bearings. The Word of Truth is our reference point to understand the grace, mercy, goodness, and righteousness of God.[57] God the Father did not just give us the written Word; He also sent us the Living Word. Jesus is the path to our spiritual destiny; He is our earthly road trip to God's supernatural realm. The revelation of God's eternal purposes shines on us through the earthly life of our Lord Jesus Christ.[58]

He is not just a prototype, God the Father wants us to breathe Jesus as our Way, Truth, and Life. Since Jesus died for all of us, we should no longer live for ourselves but for Him who died for us and was raised again. Jesus took the 100% of our sin so that through Him we can have His 100% righteousness. Therefore, we must now by faith appropriate the result of Christ's crucifixion and resurrection and breathe His life into our entire soul. Apostle Paul said,

> *I have been crucified with Christ; it is no longer I who live, but Christ lives in me; and the life which I know live in the flesh I live by faith in the Son of God, who loved me and gave Himself for me. I do not set aside the grace of God; for if righteousness comes through the law, then Christ died in vain.*
>
> *Galatians 2:20-21 NKJV*

Walk Ye in Him

Sticking with Jesus as our earthly divine road trip is the only way.[59] Jesus our Way has no detour. He is straightforward, what you see is what you get. Any road that does not bear signs of His character is not the road that will complete our soul's spiritual destiny on earth.

Religion may prophetically claim that Jesus is their prophetic way, but unless the testimony of Jesus is marked out in such a path, it is pathetic and not prophetic at all. If the signs of God's government and dominion are not evident, asserting Jesus as their apostolic way defeats their very statement.

Jesus as the God's sole divine image for sonship is our connecting way to the Father. As believers of the Gospel, Jesus is the truth that our faith lives. He is the basis of our freedom.

Everything else enslaves and subjugates. Our life in Christ is the sole source of our life's importance, and everything else is just a whirlpool that sucks out substance.

The truth is absolute; it is an entire completion. Nothing satisfies our uncertainties but Jesus. The truth is not just a condition; it is the Person. It is the Lord Jesus Christ Himself. Presently, God is telling us; "Jesus - My Son is the Way, walk ye in Him."[60]

The Keys of the Kingdom

There is a door in between our life's faith episodes, an entry way where we exit the old. The good news is Jesus has already given us the Keys of the Kingdom; that whatever is already opened in Heaven we have keys to open it up on earth. Whatever is already shut in heaven, we have the keys to shut it down on earth.

> *And I will give you the keys of the kingdom of heaven, and whatever you bind on earth will be bound in heaven, and whatever you loose on earth will be loosed in heaven."*
>
> Matthew 16:19 NKJV

The entrance, the inheritance, and the manifestation of the Kingdom of God require spiritual keys to experiencing it. Through revelation knowledge, the Spirit of God supplies us with keys of the Kingdom. Here are some (but not limited to) lists of the keys of the Kingdom:

- The Name of Jesus
- The Blood of Jesus
- The door of the utterance of the Gospel
- The gift of righteousness of God in Christ
- The fruit of the Holy Spirit
- The gifts of the Spirit
- The call of God
- The Faith of God
- The Grace of God
- The Forgiveness of God
- The Hope of God's calling
- The Unity of the Spirit
- The Word of God
- The Glory of God

When the revelation of the Truth is received, one's divine identity advances and his heart, and his lips reverberate new songs of the Kingdom. The revelation that Simon received from the Heavenly Father broke him through from being Simon to Jesus' prophetic affirmation of his divine destiny – Peter – "the rock upon the Rock."

There is no spiritual breakthrough without the revelation of the Word. To break through, you need keys that get you through from where you currently are unto the completion of your God's divine assignments.

CHAPTER SIX
Hard-Wired for Breakthrough
Breaking through is our default settings

Naturally Hard-Wired for Growth

Encoded within an inseminated life is a synergized potential of a maternal and a paternal DNA. From its inception, integral processes of its nature are stages of embryonic breakthrough. Truly, in every tiny human lifeform is a fascinating ability to carry out its growth and maturation; it has an incredible capacity to become its fullness. An existence that began as an inseminated life is also designed to crests.

Our life does not commence when we were physically born into this world. Our life started when we were procreated through the union of our father's sperm cell and our mother's egg cell. The Christian claim that life initially exists at the time of conception confirms that procreation is the one of the main purposes of marriage between man and woman. Therefore, abortion is a crime of murdering an innocent life.

As the human lifeform began to develop on the inside, so is the host's outward display of hormonal fluctuations and ongoing body mass transformations. What is taking place on the inside is also what progressively swelling up on the outside. When the host's water breaks out, what commences next is the breaking through of the child into the world.

What awaits a birthed child is his/her life-long breakthrough stages of growth and progression. Certainly, there will be significant growing pains that will come along the way, but they are just part of where a child must go through to get him to his growth development.

Inescapably, some aching process is essentially involved in practically realizing our potential. From the outset, its alien-like image is a far cry compared to its peaked of becoming.

Growth is not a conversion; for it is in all aspects, a process. On the contrary, conversion is instantaneous; it is the initial point where growth is process. We do not have the option of circumventing our way to bypass how life sorts itself out.

The entire purpose of growing is to discover learning and maturity that await us on the next segment of life. Quest after quest, we transition to become what we are born to be.

If natural life is hard-wired with series of breakthroughs such as conception, progressive embryonic change, birth, and physical development; then it is also commendable to assert that breakthrough is an integral part of our spiritual life in Christ.

Believer's DNA – "Divine Nature Attributes"

> *"This is the new covenant that I will make with my people on that day, says the Lord, I will put my laws into their hearts, and I will write them on their minds." Then He says, I will never again remember their sins and lawless deeds."*
>
> *Hebrews 10:16-17 NLT*

Per scientists who dissected his brain, they claimed that Albert Einstein's only used 10% of his brain capacity throughout his lifetime. This is just a mental capacity of man that we are talking about; can you begin to imagine what God can accomplish through us if we would ever come to the 100% of our spiritual capacity in Christ?

Chapter 6: Hardwired for Breakthrough

We have not scratched the whole surface yet regarding all that Jesus accomplished in His crucifixion and His resurrection. A moment of revelation from the Father is better than countless hours of doing things on our own.

Relationship with Christ is better than the agony of religion. It is effortlessly easy when our divine earthly assignments are carried out in the realm of God's Spirit, for it thus produces a lasting impact.

The reality of our spirituality in Christ is beyond what our soul's limited comprehension can describe it. Apostle John stressed out that it is humanly impossible to depict everything that Jesus did in 3-1/2 years of His earthly ministry; even if we're able to write everything that Jesus taught and did, the whole earth would not be able to contain all the books that we can put in writing. In short of four years, our Lord Jesus brought down the revelation of heaven's eternity on earth.

Regarding Abraham, God's revelation about him fathering many tongues and nations was beyond what he can naturally imagine. It took Abraham many years to realize that he needed to go past human inclination in helping God out in bringing out what the Lord has promised him.

Our minds delayed understanding of the revelation of the Holy Spirit can also be a God's opportunity where He process His dealing with our soul's spirituality.

The revelation of His grace is what primes our spirituality to explode His glory. As we let the Holy Spirit guides us, the glimpse of His amazing plan will enlighten our understanding eyes.

We must all understand that it takes the Holy Spirit's guided wisdom to understand and apply the Spirit given illumination.[61]

The Holy Spirit's revelation regarding the life eternal that God the Father has graced us in Christ can release us to be the manifestation of God's glory on earth. However, associated with our launching to be the expression of God's will to this world is the process that we called - the transformation of our soul.

God's provisioning part of the transaction as far as Christ's redemption is concerned, is already a completed deal. Nevertheless, our soul's part of the bargain of understanding and receiving the reality of Christ's redemption is still in an on- going process.

Regeneration and transformation are two different things. In the Kingdom of God, our spirit was regenerated by the Spirit instantaneously, On the other hand, our soul is progressively transforming into the same image of Christ's glory as the Holy Spirit increasingly shines the heart of God towards us.

The reality of Jesus' redemptive accomplishments is all currently predisposed in our relationship with God. (Pause right here and ask God to illumine your mind regarding this statement.) To tap into the manifestation of what Jesus has achieved for us however, our soul must spiritually breakthrough into the revelatory understanding of such truth. In Christ, our spiritual condition and position are overwhelmingly available. Christ's completed redemption and eternal life are a settled reality within our regenerated spirits.

Breaking through into the realization of God's divine plan for our lives is the capacity that we are potentially ready to launch ourselves off in Christ. We can now turn this world upside down since God's eternal purpose is already imprinted in our spiritual DNA.

Floodgates of God's supernatural realm opens its divine flow into our natural world when we let our recreated spirits invade our minds. Once our focus is the Word of God and our ways are the revelation of the Holy Spirit, deploying God's heaven on earth comes typically supernatural. We are on the same platform with Him when God touches our hearts with the revelation of His purpose.

Drawing out from the Holy Spirit's leadership and revelation of God's Word secures our awareness of the mind of Christ. When our soul come to the spiritual understanding of God's settled eternity within us; mobilizing our efforts, time, and resources toward the realization of our destiny are just the normal outflow of who we are in Christ.

Walking on God's Preconfigured Good Works

> *For we are his workmanship, created in Christ Jesus unto good works, which God hath before ordained that we should walk in them.*
>
> *Ephesians 2:10 KJV*

In most suspense movies, we are left alone clueless until the twist of the story drops its payload of truth close to the conclusion of the narrative. Thereafter, our perspective shifted into a full understanding and unreserved admiration of the story.

When it comes to our spirituality in Christ, the twist of our life's story transpired at the very heart of God, way before everything else was created.

What God has graciously given us in Christ, enables us to believe, receive, and participate with His will. The word 'workmanship' mentioned in Ephesians 2:10 is the Greek word 'poema' meaning 'poem.'

Back in the eternity past, when God foresaw where you impeccably fitted with His plan; in detail, He continually narrated and recited you as His masterpiece poem before the angelic host. He spoke of you and your preordained life's purpose in Christ again and again.

> *For by grace you have been saved through faith, and that not of yourselves; it is the gift of God, not of works, lest anyone should boast. For we are His workmanship, created in Christ Jesus for good works, which God prepared beforehand that we should walk in them.*
>
> *Ephesians 2:8-10 NKJV*

We can find the Magna Carta of Christian belief in Ephesians 2:8-10. Salvation is in Christ alone, by grace alone, and through faith alone. These spiritual dynamics are outside of what human can boast to perform.

Salvation is the gift of God's grace; therefore, only faith can receive and express it. From start to finish, grace and faith are the whole essences of our spirituality in Christ. However, Ephesians 2:8-9 is not an all-comprising view without throwing verse 10 into the mix.

Eternally speaking, Ephesians 2:10 is telling us that we are already God's masterpiece. Experientially, however, we manifest both to the heavens and to the whole world that we are indeed God's masterpiece when we engage our faith to good works that God had already mapped out for us in advance.

Walking on the preconfigured good works that God the Father deposited into our spirit can only be operated in Christ alone, by grace alone, and through faith alone.

The life of grace through faith is not walking in ignorance or living in hopeless abandon. Our soul becomes who we already are in Christ in the spirit by way of revelation of the reality of what and why Christ came into this world. When our soul lines up with who we already are in Christ, we then become a living soul for God.

Our spirit is God conscious, our soul is self-conscious, and our body is world conscious. When the Holy Spirit's shed love in our hearts invades our self-conscious soul, then the same love that transformed our soul will be the same love that will be extended to the world.

Have you seen the sequence? It started from the spirit where God's awareness gushes out, then it extends to our soul where we discover ourselves in Christ, and ultimately it manifests in the flesh where the glory of Christ on us shines to the world. Our soul is a go-between.

Our soul can express the life of God (meaning; we become a living soul) when our heavenly position in Christ fuses with our earthly existence. The transformation of our soul is what keeps our physical body from expressing who we are in Christ.

When self-entitlement is abandoned and denied in exchange to what Christ's redemption has entitled us with, then our earthly expression is the faith of the Son who loved us and gave His life for us.

Salvation is not just a settled position of our recreated spirits; it is also an internal core condition where our faith derives its function. Spirituality is our eternal position and functional affirmation; it operates in grace, faith, and God's predisposed good works in Christ.

There is no way we can regard the value without considering the essential. For example, A body without a spirit is dead. The spirit is the essence in which the body can demonstrate the core of life.

The essentiality of the spirit is what outlines our body's defined value. Grace and faith are what gives value to our service in Christ.

In the life of grace, there are still works to be manifested, but it is not a kind of effort that is humanly sanctioned and instigated. It is a service expressed through revelation, conviction, and faith's corresponding action.

Grace is what Christ has done for us and faith is God's divine revelation that enables us to embody everything that Christ's blood represents. The synergy of grace and faith enables us to walk in God's foreordained purpose. Grace and faith equip us to fulfill our destiny in Christ.

Divinely Setup

> *Oh yes, you shaped me first inside, then out; you formed me in my mother's womb. I thank you, High God—you're breathtaking! Body and soul, I am marvelously made! I worship in adoration—what a creation! You know me inside and out, you know every bone in my body; You know exactly how I was made, bit by bit, how I was sculpted from nothing into something. Like an open book, you watched me grow from conception to birth; all the stages of my life were spread out before you, The days of my life all prepared before I'd even lived one day.*
>
> Psalm 139:13-16 The Message

Our spiritual identity is inherent within our recreated spirit; it is who we are, what we have, and what we can do in Christ. By engaging our faith with His exceeding, great, and precious promises, our soul experientially participates with God's divine nature.

Central to our soul's spiritual breakthrough is our interface with God and His plan; this is the only way we can be set apart from the influence of the fallen world.

Though "in part" we presently operate in God's dimension, and "in part" we have a revelation of the eternal, but deep inside our spirit - the complete epitome of the righteousness of God is divinely positioned and assigned.

The only reason why the Bible ascribed our earthly engagement with the Divine as "in part," it is all because our finite mind has no full temporal description yet of what our eternal position in Christ is. The only thing that is keeping us from letting God transfigure the temporary unto eternal is our unrestored mind. The key to His Coming is the glorious mind renewal of the bride.

What releases us to our fullness in Christ is our fully restored soul. In Christ, we are whole within our spirit, but in regards with our soul; we are still inconsistent compare to our recreated spirit in Christ.

We are still in the process of putting parts of the puzzle together if you please. From one spiritual revelation at a time, we are in an ongoing manner of breaking out to become in our soul whom we already are in our recreated spirit in Christ.

When our soul is, enlightened and synchronized with Lord's plan, we are putting on God's envisioned new man that enforces God's authority over the earth.

Written Default Settings

In web development, written scripts at the framework level specify lists of variables that regulate the website's behavior. A web page consistently functions within its coded values.

In the event of mousing-over or mouse clicking a hyperlink, a specified default setting hidden in the background is triggered to kick in; meaning, a predetermined connection is executed, and it then shifts you to an explicit internet site destination.

In the same manner, the flow of Rivers of Living Water is hard-wired in our divine nature attributes – spiritual DNA. For instance, in God's time and season, a human need can supernaturally link up with God's plan when we obey the prompting of the Holy Spirit; and that is, we rendezvous with the whole intention of God in our life's specified season.

Picking up a divine prompting from the Holy Spirit brings the hand of God in the heart of someone who desperately need His touch. Such is the way we break new grounds and recognizes every unrealized good thing that we have in Christ Jesus.

The treasure within our earthen vessel is the framework where our faith navigates the supernatural landscapes that we are hard-wired within.

The actualities of the eternal redemption that the Lord Jesus Christ completed and perfected for us are all predisposed on the tablets of our born-again spirits. We are complete in Him, who is the Head of all principalities and power.

We are wholly satisfied when we are fascinated and absorbed with our God-given purpose. There is nothing more heaven like on earth than being in God's plan for our soul.

Tapping into our Wiring Stream Sequence

In 1993, I spoke at a Catholic Charismatic service at Santa Maria local Parish Church in Paco, Manila. As I entered the church, the Lord spontaneously flashed me a vision of a white dove holding a double-edged sword.

I unenthusiastically probed and reasoned with God; "Are you going to perform a miracle here? It is a Catholic Church! Can't you see these life-sized idols around?"

I rather had God turn His miracle up in my preferred venue – my local church. We deserve to receive more because we are not idol worshippers; we are a "Full Gospel Church." Today as I looked back, we were worse than these Catholic brethren, because we vainly worship our full Gospel status with pride.

It amazes me to understand that God does not perform miracles based on our merits and classifications. His love and His grace recognize no distinction. I learned two valuable lessons that night. First, God's love cannot be bound by religious labels. Secondly, God's incredible power works in any environment and any condition!

Every time God reveals His intention; He speaks it in the default setting where we can flow with the Holy Ghost. Our spiritual wiring stream sequence is initially a revelation that shines in our spirit, illuminated in our soul, and then manifestation in the physical realm. Externally, nobody can demonstrate a steadfast passion without a solid inward revelation.

I quietly backed down and said these words; "Okay Lord, if this is what you want me to do, I am willing to do it!" When I stood up to preach the Gospel, in transition, I declared the revelation that I saw; "Tonight!" I told them, "God is going to perform great things in our midst!" At the end of my speech, an old man came forward in response to a word of knowledge concerning a deaf ear that God supernaturally touched that night. By faith, I placed both of my index fingers in the old man's ears and commanded the spirit of deafness to leave in the name of Jesus. When I released my fingers, Sister Noemi Manansala, who was watching everything as she stood with me in prayer, saw a dark entity came out from one of the old man's ears, and it fell to the floor and crawled out of the church.

Later, Sister Noemi Manansala told me that she also smelled a foul odor coming from that demon and it made her ran towards the church's window and threw up. Praise God! The old man was delivered from that deaf spirit that night! Glory to God!

For more than six years, I was their weekly resident speaker. At the opening of the seventh year, they all came to me and took me to the back of the church and showed me a truck load of idols. They renounced all their idol graven images, started a Bible church of their own which produced satellite churches in different places.

A well-meaning time and season of ministry with these Catholic brethren which the Lord entrusted me, concluded in the seventh year. Hallelujah!

In its full potential, our God-given destiny is inherently hard-wired within our recreated spirits; the degree of the dedication we allow in our lives determines the dynamics towards the realization of what the Holy Spirit is capable of manifesting through us.

The grace of God is free but anointing always has a price tag – the price of consideration of self as dead to self-entitlement.[62] Through a series of learning curves, I realized that; first, the voice of God is always for the greatest end. Secondly, the voice of reason often gratifies selfish desire.

What Drives Our Perspective?

As Plato said, "...beauty is in the eye of the beholder." It is amazing to realize that people can look differently at the same thing. Our perspective in life is either driven by an influence coming from the external world or the revelation that emerges from the Holy Spirit within.

Chapter 6: Hardwired for Breakthrough

God's ordained sequence of our existence is in the order of spirit, soul, and body. Reversing this arrangement leads only to an inferior perspective of living. We manifest peace and life eternal when we live life from the inside going out. On the contrary, confusion and corruption are results of a life lived from the outside going in. Apostle Paul says;

> *For those who live according to the flesh set their minds on the things of the flesh, but those who live according to the Spirit, the things of the Spirit.*
>
> *Romans 8:5 NKJV*

Through the new birth, the Holy Spirit has written sequence of divine nature on the tablet of our hearts. Our external activity is ordained to propel from this internal new creation identity. Life is either reacting based on the impressions from outside coming in or responding to every challenge in life based on who we are in Christ on the inside.

Struggling in life stems from the "outside going in" notion of living. If we operate our lives outside the sustaining supply of the Holy Spirit, discerning spiritual assaults against our faith's stance is difficult to control if not impossible. Living in the grace of God is made possible by constant flowing with the Spirit of grace.

The third person of the Trinity keeps us occupied with the reality of God's invisibility. The Holy Spirit is our Divine Helper and Enabler.

Negotiating our spirituality in a world absorbed with contradictions is unbearable without the constant infilling of the Holy Spirit. Spirituality is only viable by the Holy Spirit's ongoing infilling and revelation. Our total dependence on the Spirit of God decides a successful Christian living.

Our life on earth is all about what dominates our perspective. What our minds and emotions converge on is what becomes our life's viewpoint. The questions that always confronts us are: "Where do we build our soul's persona?" Is it on shifting sand of the worldly system or deep on the solid ground of the Word? Is God in control of us or are we being driven by something else?

From the Outside In

The grace of God does not nullify the will of man; it rather empowers it. Though the wind pushes the sails, yet the one who handles the helm controls the direction of the sailboat. What settles the outcome is always hinges on where we place our choices on.

The critical factor that denies us or slows us down is not our external condition, because proportionally to the direction of our perspective is what we manifest in our lives.

The prerogative is set right before our eyes; they are perspectives of: life or death,[63] blessing or curse[64], breakthrough or breakdown.[65] Our life is all up to where we submit our will. When we yield our will to God's will, God takes care of the tab from then on.

An explosion blasts when critical mass goes beyond its threshold. What suddenly goes off externally is what has been raging on the inside for some time. Now these works both ways; positive or negative.

When you are so absorbed with God's revelation for a specified time, a divine explosion of His glory may suddenly go off where heaven is touching your earth.

In the same token, when a water down perspective from the external world simmers our imagination with annoyance, do not be surprised that an emotional outburst will suddenly come into play. We lose the handle so to speak because we let circumstances of life control our thoughts and emotions.

When we cut a tomato plant from its roots, the plant died from that point even though residues of moisture will still show on its trunk, branches, and leaves.

When we got born again, we were totally cut off from old sinful nature by the precious blood of Jesus. Nevertheless, the said old nature left behind sinful residues posturing as fortified strongholds engraved deep in our soul's subconscious. They are our unrenewed soul's automatic formed tendencies.

Strongholds are a sequence of systemic dispositions that are taking residence in our soul. Strongholds influence our decision making, conversation, and actions.

These inclination forms launch corrosive attitudes of self-preservation and self-entitlement. Such predisposition form factors encapsulate our reasoning, imagination, and volition with tempers that rides on the surf of carnal sentiments.

Here are some examples of these forms:

Boomeranging

Mostly, we throw to others the judgment that we already judged ourselves out. Yes, we reflect the nagging sentiments that have been simmering within our hearts. Judgment is always an act of extending the immensity of our own "visual log" to someone else's "speck of dust."

Handing over our sentence of others is a stronghold that might have been a lifelong self-condemnation within our soul. Judging is more of projection of our personal guilt to others.

We tend to evaluate ourselves with our intentions and judge others by their actions. Take note, every time we incorrectly regard others; it comes back to us in a multipliable measure.[66]

What we sow in single measure gains in compounding portions. When we unleash a form of judgment, it boomerangs back to us plenteously.

Simon Syndrome

Are we amusing ourselves with the ambiance of 'in denial' when being confronted with the truth? Simon Peter thrice disowned his association with the Master because of his intense fear of man.

Disentangling from a lie is difficult when our state of mind is deeply rooted in self-preservation. This form of self-entitlement would rather deny the uncompromising truth as opposed to ditching the romanticized grandeur of self-delusion.

But then again, can we make a circle out of a solid square without breaking it? Certainly, not! There is a vast difference between "hyping" things up and being real.

Admittance is different from recognition. We might be aware of our condition, but we can be still in denial of it. Acknowledging our soul's true condition is linked from a firm conviction of the truth.

We are adept to accountability when we are willing to stand naked in front of the truth. When we embrace the understanding of the truth, it opens our hearts unto a life of gratefulness towards God.

Only the truth diffuses bondages of deception. Only the truth defines freedom! Only the truth enables us to live in the grace of God.[67]

Get Away Drivers

When a liability is critically exposed, diverting accountability is a common tendency. This form of shame seems to be a good getaway car in escaping expectations from responsibility. Avoiding the premise of responsibility is the primary motivation behind this insanity.

Shame drove Adam to use Eve in repelling God's conscience splitting inquiry. Shame is deeply rooted in pride.

There is nothing to be embarrassed in recognizing our limitations; there is though, with our denial of it. Our admittance of our susceptibility allows Christ's grace to consummate our soul to restoration.

Shame is an accommodation that constantly fools us around. When we acknowledge that we are weak, then such sense of needing for help liberates us from pride.

Our acknowledgment of our need of Christ frees us from our excuses. We come to complete turnaround when we fully recognize that Christ alone can cover our nakedness.

Rationing Excuses

To recruit allies to their sentiment, some runs around handing out their rationalized alibis. Esteeming excuses over the truth is a slippery slope that leads to self-deception. Burying an inescapable guilt with self-justification would not get rid of loopholes.

It is rather a quicksand that drowning us into the depths of relentless carnality. When we try to accommodate our illusion by pruning the truth, it is nothing but a bogus reflection.

When it comes to reasoning out our defenses, it is amazing how we get so foolishly creative. The problem is, there is no way we can solve our dilemmas with the same method of madness we used when we initially caused them.

Self-justification is an effort of twisting reality. The more we excuse ourselves in the light of the truth, the more we cover our messiness one on top of the other. Suiting our illusion of reality while we ignore the confrontation of the truth dissipates our energy to inevitable defeat.

Darkness does not affect light, what transforms our life of misery is the radiance of His glory. Lies do not have an impact on the truth. However, God's integrity changes human uncertainties. We cannot exclude the truth; the truth encompasses us. We cannot purge the truth; the truth cleanses us.

We will not perceive the crucial when we are preoccupied with inconsequential. Only the truth of Christ is where we can find the meaning to our identity; it is the stable platform where our faith can stand.

Overdose of Exaggeration

A confused wife told her spouse; "...every time I take this prescription pill, my tongue tells me they're getting bitterer." The husband candidly responded, "I'm sorry to hear that my dear, your tongue is evidently suffering from the ailment of exaggeration. The truth is it is just a placebo!"

As always, exaggerations are triggered by an unruly tongue. Vanity overwhelms someone who plunges himself into the depths of overestimation. Solomon said, "...in the multitude of words, sin is not lacking."[68]

An exaggeration is a form of a defense mechanism that camouflages a sense of inadequacy. It is a conventional outlet that artificially strives to fill up what is seemingly lacking. As pathetic as it can get, setting up an accomplishment on a pedestal "evang-elastically speaking" is nothing but equalizing reality with a lie. We can all agree that there is an excessive Hollywood on the ones who gauge their status based on external vanity.

Compensating for deficiency puffs the head up and shrinks the heart's handling capacity for spirituality. A conceited flare is a swelled ego built on the house of cards. It is a ticking time bomb; it sets off a self-destruct count down sequence when its sense of security is pinned down. Any persuasion that does not lead to continual proliferation is an unsubstantiated stance.

Seeking completion outside God's perfection is unattainable. Our all-time recognition should be "without Christ we are nothing, and we can do nothing." We can only find our completion in Christ. More so, plugging in our wholeness within the parameter of who we are in Christ impacts others around us as well as ourselves.

Our identity in Christ is our springboard for our faith's activity. We cannot let Christ lives His life on us without knowing that we are in Him.

These form examples - boomeranging, Simon syndrome, get away drivers, rationing excuses, an overdose of exaggeration - are deep-seated soulish strongholds that set us off to think, decide, and act along the surfs of carnal impulses of the flesh.

They are the preconceived schemas of the unrenewed mind. In review, these discoursed forms are a description of one-track mind inclinations. Their sole focus is nothing but self-entitlement. They always come with a territory.

They are tendencies that can easily lead one to frustration whenever its hidden agendas, selfish interest, and unscriptural self-image is exposed by essentiality of growth.

Fighting sin by way of patronizing the strength of the flesh will never culminate in winning. Contending against our soul's resident strongholds by natural strength is not a win-win proposition because you cannot fight carnality with your fleshly strength.

Knives are neither good nor bad; it can cut veggies, or it can be used to stab people. In the same way, our flesh can be an instrument of righteousness, or it can be a means to propagate corruption.

When it comes to spirituality, our flesh has no strength of its own. Therefore, overcoming temptation through the effort of the flesh is not only difficult, but it is impossible.

The only way we can break and demolish strongholds that are still hanging out as a residue of sin in our soul (mind, emotion, and will) is to walk in the Spirit. Jesus emphatically said; "…the flesh is weak.[69]" Nonetheless, we as believers of Christ can live above these forms, when we thrive…

From the Inside Out

> But this is the covenant that I will make with the house of Israel after those days, says the Lord: I will put My law in their minds, and write it on their hearts; and I will be their God, and they shall be My people.
>
> Jeremiah 31:33 NKJV

The New Covenant is the era where God engraved the law of His love on the tablet of our born-again spirits and against such life, the external demands of the Mosaic Law that were designed to put us in bondage are inconsequential.[70]

There is contrast between light and darkness, but the latter has no power to undo the former. Instead the light influences the darkness; yes, light shines more in darkness.

There is nothing in Mosaic Law that can be used against the Holy Spirit and His fruit. Rather, the essence of the Spirit impacts life beyond man's adherences to the Mosaic Law.

The New Covenant is the period wherein our new creation spirit relates with God. The New Covenant centers around the results of Jesus' redemptive work that was stamped on the spirits of the redeemed.

The New Covenant is the new creation life flowing from the inside out. Eternal life is a settled spiritual state of every born-again child of God. Therefore, any temporary external fixations will not gratify the eternity within our hearts.

Only the Eternal satisfies the temporal. Only the greater completes the lesser. Only the spirit contains the natural. We maximize our existence when we flow from the inside out.

The New Covenant is the dispensation of God's grace proliferated and confirmed by the power of the Holy Spirit. Yes, as our soul come into the alignment with all that Jesus accomplished on the cross and His resurrection where the flow of spiritual fellowship between God and His chosen ones can be demonstrated to the world.

Only in Christ, we can manifest the preloaded divine destiny within our spirits. When we flow in the spirit of prayer based on the Holy Spirit's revelation, the effect of such spirit led activity is beyond what our natural ability can make out of.

The Lord considers life at the precise spot where issues of life start – our heart. Tender-heartedness and sensitivity to God's dealings confirm our soul's fellowship with God. Synchronizing our soul with the law of Spirit of life that all written up within our new creation spirit unravels God's divine flow.

The Word of God is our window to these heart's divine inscriptions. His Word tells us what is up in the realm of the spirit. His Word is our perfect platform where we see life just like God Almighty sees it.

Righteousness is not just a part of our new creation reality. We never grow in righteousness; it is who we already are in Christ. Through and through, we are the righteousness of God in Christ Jesus. We are who we are in Christ.

External life starts to change when we flow our life in Christ from within. Jesus said,"…out of your innermost being shall flow rivers of living water."[71] The work of God sets off from within, and it then spreads out.

Here are some examples of "from the inside out" inherent divine flow written on the tablet of our new creation spirit in Christ:

Revelation

> *The entrance and unfolding of your words give light; their unfolding gives understanding (discernment and comprehension) to the simple.*
>
> *Psalms 119:130 Amplified Version*

When God make Himself known to us, we then realize our life's purpose. God, our Father, is the very reason of our existence. Life will not mean anything without Him.

We come to know who we are as we come to understand God through Christ Jesus and His redemption; life is purposeless apart from this revelation!

Every time the Holy Spirit unveils the mind of Christ, layers of human limitation falls off from our soul's understanding eyes. God defining moment shines on our lives as the Father personally share His heart with us.

What breaks the yoke of bondage (stronghold) that is illegally squatting in our soul is the revelation of Christ - the Anointed One.

Revelation affects us personally and relationally. It touches us because His revelation equips us with faith that rendezvous with our divine destiny.

It relationally transforms our soul, because when we engage the given revelation to a commitment of faith, our soul's fellowship with God is fine tuned.

We come to the recognition that only His unconditional love secures our standing with Him. All subsequent relationships are taken care of when our divine connection with the Father is fine tuned.

Revelation is God speaking to us; it is our divine encounter with the Father. Every time God speaks His Word, something creative and compelling is shifted into our world. The receipt of His revelation is the time and the season where faith – God's divine enablement is generated.

Positioning our God's kingdom rights and inheritance over any earthly contradiction is impossible without divinely given faith (or revelation). Revelation is the faith that enables us to walk on the supernatural.

We have nothing to offer the world without divinely granted faith – a measure of a heavenly revelation which allows us to break through impossible thing on earth. Faith is a divinely given revelation; it equips us to negotiate our heavenly citizenship on our earthly existence.

Revelation bridges the gap between heaven and earth. Heaven's Kingdom and will, will not turn up unless faith (the personal revelation of God) on earth is activated.

Revelation is the key that unlocks the manifestation of God's Kingdom on earth. Revelation is our heavenly handle where we live out Christ's resurrection power on our earthly existence.

Does it intrigue you that every blessing of God's grace has already been ratified and completed by the shed blood of Jesus and yet it is still our heavenly mandate to release it is through faith's expressions: prayer, praise and worship, thanksgiving, and divine sanctioned actions? Understanding this mystery helps us engage our identity with our divine destiny.

Revelation defines our purpose and shifts our lives to the higher dimension. Renewed devotion is an outflow of fresh reception of God's revelation.

God's part is to impart revelation; man's involvement comprises of its reception and maturation. Just like salvation is part of God's grace, faith's part is the reception of the salvation experience.

We realize the real value of revelation when our lives increase over it. From being a reed like life that can be easily swayed by circumstances, Simon's receipt of Christ's revelation forever shifted his life.[72]

Jesus said; "…upon this rock – the revelation of His Anointing - I will build My Church."[73] The divine realization of Christ makes us aware that gates (portals) of hell will never ever prevail against the Church.

The Bride of Christ will never reach her full definition and maturity without the revelation of who her Head is. God's divine orchestration will be seen on earth when by revelation each part of Christ's Body function with their God-given calling. The habitation of God on earth is being built together by us coming to our respective full measure of Christ.[74]

Revelation causes us to walk in the light as He is in the light. As the opening of God's Word awakens the eye of our soul's understanding, the revelation of His goodness illuminates the remainder of our soul's dark regions.

Such encounter of His goodness is His empowering grace for repentance (or mind renewal). Revelation is the light of the glorious knowledge of Christ that liberates our minds unto spiritual freedom.[75]

Revelation is our divine direction, a prophetic vision of what our destiny shall one day be. It is the unveiling of the God's foreordained good works - His divine assignments for us to walk through.

From faith to faith, the revelation of God's Word progressively fuses our recreated spirit into our soul's persona, so, in the end, we become God's matured living soul. Without prophetic revelation, people are defenseless and out of control.[76]

The unveiling of what God can see through time shifts our life from mere trending unto a purposeful living. When we have God's now-word (divine revelation), it is the new things of God where it serves us an exit door from life's challenges and circumstances. The new thing is our transitioning phase from the old.

The revelation has a weight of God's eternal glory. It comes in the form of spontaneous flashes of images, inward impressions, and unexplained train of thoughts.

On some occasion, it is a word from the scripture that comes alive as it is being read or being heard preached. Revelation is hearing the voice of God.[77]

The Intriguing Question

The question that confronts us now is; "is a revelation knowledge a mystery to our new creation spirit?" Here is what Apostle Paul said;

Therefore, if anyone is in Christ, he is a new creation; old things have passed away; behold, all things have become new. Now all things are of God...

2 Corinthians 5:17-18a NKJV

2 Corinthians 5:17-18 tells us that all the attributes of the new creation spirit are of God. The old sinful nature is no longer a part of our born again spirit. The new things of our recreated spirits are ALL from God. Our inner man now communicates a new nature.

Our recreated spirit is now completely righteous with Christ. Jesus emphatically said that the spirit that has been born again saw and entered God's Kingdom.[78]

Therefore, our new creation spirit has no need of revelation. Our soul is the one that needs revelation because it is still in the process of being completed. Revelation is indispensable to a condition that necessitates completion.

Revelation is the light that shines in the darkness. Revelation is the understanding that gives sight to our unrenewed minds. It is the truth that liberates our soul from every high thing (or idolatry) that exalts itself against God's purpose.

It is the light of God that synchronizes our soul with our new creation spirit. As our soul progressively lines up with our identity in Christ, we are steadily being transformed as a living soul ready to manifest a living sacrificed body.

Revelation has an Eternal Consequence

In the summer of 1992 in the house of a Catholic Charismatic sister in the Lord, as we closed our eyes to conclude our home Bible study in prayer, suddenly, a spontaneous vision of a set of hands flashed right in front of me. I promptly knew the Holy Spirit specifically highlighted a condition of numbing fingers.

There were just four of us at my friend's house and getting myself out of the equation, the probability that I am right on the money was two is to one. However, the inward witness of the Holy Spirit was more compelling than all of us four.

Nonetheless, in faith I declared what I saw; a brother in the Lord responded and confirmed that he was the one with such ailing hands. In Jesus' name, he received his healing that night. Hallelujah!

I know now for certain that in God's grand scheme of things, the Lord has a greater purpose in the life of that man than just his physical healing.

Obeying the Spirit of God has an eternal outcome, and it is greater than what we can ever imagine. A simple turn of an unwilling ear to hear what the Lord was saying could have change the course of that brother's life.

It is one thing to receive the revelation, and it is another thing to engage your faith after you receive the Spirit's disclosure. The scripture says, "…he who has ears to hear, LET him hear what the Spirit is saying."

Correspondingly, I was completely unaware that such occasion was a divine setup for the life of a sister whom I met for the first time that night. After she saw the Holy Spirit's revelatory manifestation, Sister Fe Buenviaje, asked me to counsel her about her pending decision to join a group tour bound for the United States where she can pursue a career opportunity.

Nonetheless, a verse of scripture came to my mind and I told her; "…let the peace of God arbitrates your heart."   I instructed her; "Don't go without sensing the peace of God inside of you." In agreement with faith, we lifted her concern in prayer.

Months later, God gave her an opportunity to receive a hand down financially challenged travel agency business from her Uncle. She took the opportunity, and God blessed it as one of the thriving traveling agencies in Manila today.

Later, she opened her business office for Bible study and fellowship. Currently, the Lord is using her as the leader of a Catholic Charismatic group in Manila, and she broadcasts a weekly radio program designed to reach Catholics for Jesus. What an amazing work of God! Hallelujah! Praise God!

Manifestation is a given when revelation is taken. A promise becomes tangibly real when a revelation is appropriated through faith in the power of the Holy Spirit.

Conviction

> *The Spirit Himself bears witness with our spirit that we are the children of God.*
>
> *Romans 8:16 NKJV*

Stepping further within our recreated spirit is essential to understand what conviction really is. What carries us beyond our natural perception is a resilient spiritual stance. On the contrary, the absence of awareness regarding our spirituality in Christ leads us to a never-ending runaround, like a dog to its own tail.

Yes, a life deficient of conviction leads to an existence of confusion. Spirituality opens our awareness further than our natural limitation.

When the realm of the Spirit is directing our earthly existence, we will surely make an undeniable narrative in our today's culture.

When we flow along the Holy Spirit's direction, we will see how the heavenly purpose written in the DNA of our born-again spirit facilitates heavenly dynamics in the place where we live, work, and hangout. What would the Body of Christ be, when we all run our lives from the unction of the Holy Spirit's conviction?

We would all certainly enforce heaven's will and God's dominion on earth. When our conviction is: Jesus is the King and the Lord over our lives, then everything that we will outflow from the inside going out is a passion that pertains to life and godliness.

We come to our true being when God personally unveils His heart to us. Revelation is God way of speaking to us and conviction is our giving account to every revelation we received from the Spirit of God.

The voice of our conviction is God's internal indicator of go or stop or proceeding with caution. Training ourselves to draw from an inward witness sustains our heart's integrity in the Straight and Narrow.

Conviction is an inward passion for the reality of the unseen realm of God. Amid prevailing negativities in this world, the Spirit of God convinces us on who we are, what we have, and what we can do in Christ.

Conviction is an inward guarantee that no matter what happens in life, God in Heaven is our Father and He will take good care of us as His dear children.

Conviction gives us the assurance that God's faithfulness is greater than all curve balls that the world can throw at us. The Bible also says; faith is the conviction of things not seen.[79] Our physical eyes may not see God's invisibility, but our conviction helps us perceived the Lord's sovereignty.

Conviction stirs us up from the inside until our earthly experience culminated to the level of what we believe. By having the conviction of God's greatness within us, we turn the tide of the world's seemingly aura of difficulty unto a great opportunity to spread His goodness.

Wisdom

How many times have we seen people with noble intention self-destruct with their uncontrolled emotion? When we are caught off guarded, commendable sentiments can suddenly distort itself unto an uncontrolled emotion.

In bad timing and at wrong places, right stuff can be an improper substance if wisdom is lacking.

Paul stated in Galatians 6:1; even a mature spiritual person, can also lose their cool through a given heated emotional argument if they are not keeping their emotions in check when he is trying to restore a fallen brother.

If we are deficient of wisdom, redirecting an adrenaline rush into a place of calmness and creativity is extremely challenging. Lacking in wisdom drives us to be swift to anger, hasty in speaking and idling in hearing.

Wisdom is Found in the Right Place at the Right Time

> *For God did not give us a spirit of timidity (of cowardice, of craven and cringing and fawning fear), but [He has given us a spirit] of power and love and of calm and well-balanced mind and discipline and self-control.*
>
> *2 Timothy 1:7 Amplified Version*

Chapter 6: Hardwired for Breakthrough

Wisdom is always right on the queue at a moment's notice. What wisdom brings to the table is a spiritual virtue that is poised with boldness, power, love, well-balanced mind, discipline, and self-control.

What facilitates the successful course of action are wisdom's right timing, right environment, and precise input.

In the secular world, to turn things out remarkably ingenious, compatible interfacing and interaction among peers must be expected. The downside of this scheme is, not everyone is exactly like you.

Human dynamics flows from different orientations, and due to personality differences and cultural uniqueness, conflict is not a chance of event but an inevitable occurrence. By wisdom, however, differences and diversities can be creatively addressed and resolved.

The flow of a spiritual virtue cannot be self-staged. Wisdom cannot go outside the life of prayer and our sensitivity to God's timing.

The mind of Christ that is sought in prayer ahead of time will always overcome weaknesses of the flesh. The wisdom grasped from God's presence launches an unlimited ability of the new creation spirit. [80]

As a newbie on my drafting job back in 2008, this mechanical engineer kept coming to my cubicle in numerous times and on different occasions. As loud as he can be, he constantly asked me about an advanced mechanical engineering discipline.

The snag was, my Trade School bare bones AutoCAD drafting training, was solely meant to assists engineers in drafting their design plots. Advanced engineering disciplines were way beyond my academic aptitude and paygrade.

After these recurring intimidations and embarrassing moments, something spontaneously popped inside of me one day. I asked him; "…you know, I have no idea about the advanced mechanical engineering discipline that you kept asking me about, but I would appreciate it if you would teach me what they are and how they work; then next time you ask me, I would surely know what and how to answer your questions."

Despite my eagerness to learn, his unwillingness to train me further, stopped him from his quest of intimidation and embarrassments. Wisdom can expose madness of foolishness in a heavy dose of kindness.

Wisdom is the key that turns the tide the other way around and puts us in control over menacing situations. Our way can weave through joy, success, and victory when God's wisdom harnesses our difficult situation into something that manifests God's divine order.

With wisdom, we can discern our way of escape even amid temptation. When we handle situations wisely, a problem becomes our workshop for creativity. Wisdom keeps us steadfast, complete, and lacking nothing. Jesus – the wisdom of God is availably ready to our soul every time we seek the guidance of the Holy Spirit.

Compassion

Back in 1992, as part of our pastoral care outreach, I visited the home of an elderly member of our local church. Minutes later after I got inside her house, the old woman's eldest son came in and disrespectfully deflected my polite greetings with sharp and snobbish attitude. Unreservedly, he made his intention known by giving me the gesture of; "I have nothing to do with you" look on his face.

While he was throwing a fit over my presence in their house, I quietly prayed and sought the mind of Christ for such occasion. Out of nowhere, I saw a vision of him crying when he is usually by himself in his bed. I waited for the right moment, and when I had my chance during the unpleasant atmosphere, without hesitation,

I shared what I saw and told him that the Lord knows his deep-seated loneliness and countless cries of anguish. Unexpectedly, like a little kid, he sobbed profusely where his tears and mucus mixed up. That night the Lord opened his heart, and he accepted Jesus as his Savior and Lord.

Even the toughest of nails, when God's compassion flows, His goodness will lead them to contrition. Regardless of man's adverse condition, God's compassion transports His offer of wholeness for man's condition of defectiveness. A divine flow of compassion can open a hardened heart and liberate such man in tearful and joyful expressions of repentance.

Compassion is God's mercy in action; it channels the heart of God through divine healing, deliverance, and miracles. The Bible says, "...Compassion moved Jesus,"[81] and He healed the sick and brought deliverance to them who were oppressed by evil spirits.

Love conquers all things. Severe conditions stand no chance against the flow of God's compassion. God's love brings freedom to all torments of fear. God's love that was shed abroad within by the Holy Spirit is a virtue that beams by those who live their faith from the inside out.

Blessing

Before man came along, God took the precedence of creating all conceivable provisions and everything that would be later discovered as a necessity for man's continuous earthly existence.

He created and put together all earth's fullness to furnish man's need as well as securing an environment where the man-Adam can express his God-given identity and authority.

The creation of man marks the completion of the entire creation, for he is the pinnacle of all that God created. When in the presence of his Creator Adam stood up his initial existence, it thus signifies that God alone constitutes his entirety.

Each time God spoke His creation into existence, the Lord conferred it with His blessings. God has His stamp of blessing on everything He created. The entire creation is maximizable to its fullest potential, that is why He called all of them GOOD after He created them.

Truly, the man under God's authority can tap all earth's elements and exploit them unto their broadest applications. They are all proficient, effective, and beneficial for something.

From His goodness, God commenced everything He created. He feels good about His job, but even more so with man, for we are His masterpiece. Adam was God's handcrafted work. He was His Spirit breathed creation, created in His image and His likeness. God's satisfaction was expressed fully, when after He had created the man Adam, He said this of him; "you are very good."[82]

Out of God's excellence, He created man; we are not designed for inferior things but only for the optimum. When Adam stood up to his feet, he entered the rest of the Lord. Adam's first day was God's seventh day of completion.

Man commenced his first day resting in communion with God. The Lord called the day as holy as He commune with man. In blessing the seventh day, man is blessed to enter God's rest. It was awesomely good!

Chapter 6: Hardwired for Breakthrough

Fast forward to where we are at now, God once and for all completed His plan of redemption for man through His Son Jesus. With the curse that His Son took upon Himself, God conferred His awesome blessings on all of us.

It is His Son who said, "It is finished!" Meaning, it is completely complete, it is perfectly perfect, in other words; "it was very good!" Now while God still calls our earthly existence as Today, let us all enter the rest of the finished work of Christ.

Jesus is our completion. We entered a spirit to Spirit relationship with God the Father through Jesus - the New and Living Way.[83] God having us in Christ means His blessings constituted us.

We cannot have Him without His blessings. We have His blessings because God has us. In Christ, God has poured into our lives all spiritual blessings in the heavenly places.[84] In Christ, God's blessing is at our disposal. Therefore, the acknowledgment of every good thing that we have in His Son-Jesus is just rightfully so.

In the same token, the power to bless our world is the authority that God placed on our shoulders. We are to enforce His blessings on this cursed world. We are to bless the world that despitefully uses us. We are mandated to overcome evil by speaking His blessings over it.

We are gutters of His awesome grace. We frame our world with God's blessing that flows from the inside and out of our mouth. Our tongue is a fountain where we can release God's blessings to our adverse situation. In Christ, we can eternally affect the life's course of an individual, family, and even a nation when we bless them.

Despite current contradiction in the natural, people of faith are hopeful of their world because they can turn around the adverse and difficult situations as they prophetically declare God's grace over them.

The rivers of blessing that flow from our innermost being can supersede the disruption of sin that abounds in the world today. We bless the undeserving; we release God's goodness on hopeless situations.

Can we all engage ourselves to be the fountain of blessings instead of a fountain of cursing? We cannot be in the middle ground. If we are not engaged, then we are not flowing from our divine connection!

Now, since the Holy Spirit engrossed us with the revelation of His goodness and grace, we can now be His participating mouthpiece. God blessed us, so we can be a blessing.

Anointing

Jesus went about spreading God's goodness and healing all who were oppressed of the devil as a Man under the anointing and power of the Holy Spirit.[85] Jesus' earthly ministry embodied what co-laboring with God is all about.

The basis of Jesus' earthly ministry was His total dependence on the guidance, leadership, and manifestations of the Spirit. Our Lord Jesus exemplified what sons of God ought to be, a life on the total dependency on the Holy Spirit.

God's Spirit indwells us to partner with us in doing the will of God. The Holy Spirit is sent to be our Helper and not our doer.

Gospel preaching and teaching is our side of the bargain, confirming it with signs and wonder is the Holy Spirit's portion of the deal. We all need the God's Spirit drawing power; the world cannot come to Jesus unless the Spirit of God enables them.[86]

A religion rigged with performance and flamboyance will not even come close to what the life in the Spirit can bring. A life triggered by the religious agenda and tradition is a predictable monotony of wearisome endeavor.

In contrast, life in the Spirit is a passion born out of God's conviction from within. It is a life that flows from the inside. It is the life carried from the wealth of our relationship with God that unleashes His provision to the world. It is the river that never runs dry as opposed to a life of struggle that leads to dryness and exhaustion.

In Jewish tradition, the word anointing depicts a portion of an ointment smeared upon a certain individual. In scriptural perspective, it describes a measured platform on which God can and will use a person to reach his sphere of influence on a level that is divinely distinctive of his calling.

Anointing is in every calling of God; it is the evidence that a man has a calling from God. Whom He appoints, He anoints.

Flowing in the Measured Anointing

But to each one of us grace was given according to the measure of Christ's gift.

Ephesians 4:7 NKJV

Jesus during His earthly mission, flowed in an immeasurable anointing of the Holy Ghost.[87] An individual believer the other hand, can only flow in ministry within his God's allocated grace. We cannot find the total measure of Christ's gift in an individual believer.

Corporately, however, the Body of Christ shares the whole measure of Christ. Corporate anointing manifests the glory of God robustly in comparison to the Holy Spirit's operation with just an individual believer.

Anointing is a shared realm of God in a measure. Why God imparts in portion? It is because we have no way of containing God's full measured anointing with our corruptible bodies. What fatally strike Ananias and Sapphira was their spiritual slackness amid the manifestation of the anointing of God.

By trying to portray a larger than life image with their staged-up generosity, they disrespected the anointing of God, and in the process, their pride was the cause why they were dispelled from the glory of God.[88]

So out of God's kindness towards us, He manifests Himself in an "in-part" way. Until the time where the earth is ready for God's entire presence where He will tabernacle among us, we'll remain in the condition of receiving the manifestation of God from glory to glory; that is, the impartation of anointing will be in segments and portion.

The Meek will Rule the Earth

At the preceding level, the handling capacity for our soul's next spiritual stage must be proven first. God's great salvation is by grace alone, through faith alone, and in Christ alone.[89] However, God's anointing is a platform where every believer who desires to live per what God called and gifted him for must dethrone self and enthrone Jesus as their Lord and King.

Again, The Answer identifies the problem with solution; the problem always points us to the means of solving its dilemma. The New Covenant scripture says, God resists the proud and gives grace to the humble. Resurrection life does not manifest in life where pride has not yet received its death blow.

Like it or not, new wine can only be poured in and poured through a renewed wineskin. Soul's brokenness is the condition where anointing can fall upon and remain.

We may have the right platform, the right church's frontline affiliation, a collection of good books, and right confession but they are all just words that is void of power if the Holy Spirit's leadership is not sought after. Earth's ownership and dominion only belong to the meek.

Revelation knowledge is the key where divine anointing enables us to open and shut things on earth that were already loosed and bound in heaven. However, our soul's meekness or sensibility to God's revelation is essential to our flowing with the Spirit's anointing.

Only a restored soul can offer up living sacrificed body that demonstrates His will. Will you be this kind of man for God? You see, we do not have anything to offer to the world until we let the Holy Spirit flows through us with His anointing.

Contingent to the Holy Spirit's Will

During my short ministerial gig in California back in 2012, I was shocked when some people asked me to set a schedule of prophetic utterances for them. I had to turn it down because it is not scriptural. More so, they just wanted to hear things that tickle their ears. I frankly responded to them; "we are opening ourselves up to occult activity when we try to manifest prophecy based on our initiative."

The Spirit of prophecy flows as the Spirit wills.[90] Flowing with the anointing is not a convenient switch that we can turn on and off to our liking. Operations of the Spirit are gifts of grace – "charisma." They do not operate through the works of man but by the Spirit of grace through faith.

We saw how the Body of Christ was wounded and hurt in the past because the authority of the scripture was not permitted to provide the check and balance on our presumed spiritual manifestations. We equated prophetic utterances as an absolute inspiration over the scriptures. Prophecies are given to confirm what God has already spoken in the heart of a believer.

In the New Covenant, we are not primarily guided by the prophets but by the Holy Spirit and His Word. Any occurrence of spiritual gifts must be in total agreement with God's Word. Divine revelation cannot supersede the authority of the Holy Scriptures.

The Word of God is our yardstick; anything that opposes the Bible is in the spirit of error. Prophecy outside the Holy Spirit is not a divine inspiration; it is rather a human perspiration motivated by religious fanaticism that leads to deception.

The Presence of God

You will show me the path of life; In your presence is fullness of joy; At your right hand are pleasures forevermore.

Psalms 16:11 NKJV

Me and my childhood friends grew up watching our favorite TV cartoon program called "Mightor". We could care less if they were countless reruns. What mattered to all of us was, we all got the kick of it whenever Mightor and Tog - his flying fire breathing dinosaur shows up in the scene and give bad guys a beating.

In our unassuming child-like curiosity, something sets our joy off to the max whenever the atmosphere of our cartoon program changed from hopelessness onto a promising victory.

In the same way, entities of darkness flee in recognition of their defeat whenever the light of God's glorious presence manifests. Every time God shows up; a localized place becomes a habitation of His Quantified Heaven.

The peace that passes all understanding becomes the natural divine order of the moment in a place where the presence of God manifests.

Wherever God shows up, the joy unspeakable and the pleasure of eternity permeates the heart of the people He touches. God is invisible, and He is beyond what our five senses can explore. Nonetheless, in the atmosphere where the manifested presence of God is standing out, there is a real conspicuous phenomenon that is way beyond reason and lingual expressions.

In 1984, I got invited to speak in a Catholic Charismatic group in a boarding house near Manila Central University. There was something vastly different in the air that night. As soon as I opened my mouth to preach the Gospel, the Lord opened my eyes, and God's presence was enveloping me like a mist of clouds. The weight of God's presence was heavy, deep conviction and God's supernatural waves flooded the dormitory's living room.

During our prayer time, as I gently laid my right hand towards a guy's forehead, his body tilted backward, and when I retracted my hand towards me, he then inclined forwardly. When I waved my hand sideward, his body leaned in the same direction. His eyes were close, and I was not even physically pushing him, and then the person behind him fell first, and this man who later went to Bible School fell sideward.

On that night, God's manifested presence convinced these Catholic brethren that He is real than their rituals and traditions. The said time and season produced fruits that remained even to this day.

The actuality of His presence is beyond what we can make of Him in our earthly existence. The immaturity of our soul's dispositions often sidetracks us from our awareness of His presence.

We have often mistaken that our religious service is the form where we worship the Father. Nonetheless, our service is just a byproduct of our worship of God.

A ministry born out of worship of God facilitate the miraculous presence of God in our sphere of influence. Worship always precedes our service. In the presence of the Almighty, God's supernatural ability for service is a given. The Lord Jesus prioritized worship over service.

We are filled by the One we worship. We spill over His divinity to the world around us when we are soaked in His presence. We become the miraculous display of the One who fills us. Impossibilities become feasibly possible when what makes the difference in our midst is His presence. The Gospel of Matthew and Mark says,

> Jesus looked at them and said, "With man this is impossible, but with GOD all things are possible."
>
> Matthew 19:26 NKJV

> ...the Lord is working with them and confirming the word through the accompanying signs. Amen.
>
> Mark 16:20 NKJV

When God's presence is in our midst, a ministry is no longer a squeezing of rivers of Living Water out of bone-dry religious tradition. Signs and wonders are light and easy flows from our innermost being. God wants us to indulge ourselves excessively with His life and with His presence. When we are full of the Holy Spirit, we become active floodgates of God's manifested presence where we gush out His blessings into the barren conditions of this world. All throughout the Bible times, those who were full of the Spirit of God validates His presence. Here are some Biblical evidences:

- We become sensitive to the Holy Spirit's leadership when we are full of the Spirit:

    Then Jesus, being filled with the Holy Spirit ... and was led by the Spirit into the wilderness... Luke 4:1 NKJV

    > Being full of the Spirit is a dimension where our spiritual sense of perceiving and discernment are deployably ready.

- We can discern the spiritual worlds when we are full of the Spirit:

    Then Saul, who also is called Paul, filled with the Holy Spirit, looked intently at him and said, "O full of all deceit and all fraud, you son of the devil, you enemy of all righteousness, will you not cease perverting the straight ways of the Lord? And now, indeed, the hand of the Lord is upon you, and you shall be blind, not seeing the sun for a time." And immediately a dark mist fell on him, and he went around seeking someone to lead him by the hand. Then the proconsul believed, when he saw what had been done, being astonished at the teaching of the Lord.   Acts 13:9-11 NKJV

- We are able to interpret dreams with wisdom when we are full of the Spirit:

    Joseph's suggestions were well received by Pharaoh and his officials. So Pharaoh asked his officials, "Can we find anyone else like this man so obviously filled with the spirit of God?" Then Pharaoh said to Joseph, "Since God has revealed the meaning of the dreams to you, clearly no one else is as intelligent or wise as you are. Genesis 41:37-39 NLT

- We are full of joy when we are full of the Holy Spirit

    And the disciples were filled with joy and with the Holy Spirit. Acts 13:52 NKJV

    > Being full of God's Spirit is the link that prime the subsequence to fall in place. He who He is, is at our disposal in Christ.

- We are filled with boldness when we are full of the Spirit:

    And when they had prayed, the place where they were assembled together was shaken; and they were all filled with the Holy Spirit, and they spoke the word of God with boldness. Acts 4:8 NKJV

    > Boldness is based on God's divine revelation and not on speculation.

    > Boldness is a divine passion that gushes out from within.

It is an Inside Job

Can we produce God's supernatural activity through our fleshly religious motions? Of course, not! God is beyond than what we can religiously make of Him. When through our traditions, we downplay God's Word and the power of God's Spirit, we shrunk our divine interaction with God with just recitals of His past's miraculous exploits.

Religion always gets settled by being struck with the reading of the letter of the law rather than having a passion of experiencing the glory of God.

Religion merely trends with status quo but those who chose to have their existence commence from the inside out, they go beyond hyping up.

The God who worked inside of us is the same Lord who desires to flow through us. What substantiated us from the inside is the same that validates us on the outside. We manifest what the Spirit of God has settled within us.

What drives us internally is what can be demonstrated externally. We trigger the operation of the new creation when we initiate life from within.

Eternal life is a settled absolute within us. Life going from the inside out enlarge boundaries. God inside us is greater than external things that try to confine us.

Demonstrating what God established in our hearts is not laborious when its operation is coming from the willingness of the spirit within and not from the external struggle of the flesh at without.

When we call deep unto deep or in other words our spirit engages with the Spirit of God, the Lord energizes our lives both to will and to do of His good pleasure.

There is no way that we can extract water out of a dry towel, we soak it first and then we can squeeze it thereafter. Trying to emanate the essence of God out of a rigid religious servitude is unnecessary and indeed a ludicrous endeavor.

A service that is independent of the presence of God is a mode of expression that is deficient of His power. Expectation secures relevant result when the environment is conducive for the Holy Spirit to move.

Revelation and Manifestation

You do err, not knowing the scriptures, nor the power of God.

Matthew 22:29 NKJV

The word "err" mentioned in the above scripture means "to roam hither and thither." It is a description of being here and there; it is a constant shifting of stance from one side and to the adjacent side; thus, it implies a shaky position.

We will not stagger in our conviction when our adherence is the Word and the revelation of the Spirit. Having one without the other sets us up in the place of vulnerability.

The compositions of a balanced faith life are the revelation of the Word of God and the demonstration of the Spirit. We cannot have one, without the other. Life in the Spirit verifies the Word of God and the Word of God authenticate life in the Spirit.

We will always be in excesses and abuses when all that we pursue is to be emotionally high in the Holy Ghost. On the other hand, if all that we have is the proclamation of the Word, we will dry out in boredom.

Faith without action does not demonstrate the life of God. A life initiated from the inside will complete itself on the outside.

What becomes our external expression is the thought that we keep on pondering. Faith is not just a proclamation of revelation; it is also a Kingdom demonstration.

Our input decides our output. Without the Word, there is nothing the Holy Spirit can demonstrate. Nonetheless, all that we have are empty words if the power of the Spirit is lacking.

Balance is the Way of Life

In the absence of balance, life will not exist. We may engross ourselves in a lifelong argument against such a statement, but the essentiality of balance is what carries us in our day to day life.

What would happen if the hubs of wheels of your car are off centered? Undeniably, weird and funny as it can get; your wheels will roll elliptically, like peaks and valley.

Whatever type of road you are on, uphill, downhill or a straight plane, driving in such an imbalanced way is cumbersome. Not to mention, due to related strain, your car's length of service will not last long.

The spin, orbit, and rotation of the star, planets and its moons, asteroids, and comets are what makes up the order of our solar system. Each gravitational element harmoniously compensates and balances the whole system out.

In a coordinated fashion, each parts of the system pulls the others in and pushes the other out. The individual movements of each element to the whole system are like a grand concerto to the ears of its Creator.

Balance is what keeps our solar system intact. The function of each part is vital to the whole structure. If somehow the movement of every part of the system becomes identical, violent disintegrations of the entire system is inevitable.

The allocation of each distance, movements, and designated gravitational push and pull are what offsets each other out; it is what makes our solar system unbroken and operational.

We always find balance in every aspect of life. Even in healthy living, balance distribution of food intake is a must. Balance in our breathing pattern and even physical movements is also imperative.

What makes you think that we all have two eyes, two ears, two feet, two hands and with only one mouth, balance! We have nights and days, low and high tides. Now, if a balance is vital and significant in every spectrum of life, have we asked ourselves what balances our spiritual living?

Growth Takes Care of Balance

Balance is a given when there is a growth process. It is not a head-scratcher to say that lack of growth is a symptom of a spiritual imbalance. Balance is taking care of when we grow up spiritually,

The big question is, "how we can gauge growth that is indicative of a balanced spiritual life?" For a starter, any spiritual dynamics that has an eternal consequence is a good measuring stick.

The scripture says that understanding, gifts, calling, and knowledge will all pass away and the only spiritual virtue that will last forever is love. Compassion is the measuring stick of growth. The love of God is what balances us all.

Faith is imbalance without the revelation of the love of God. We love because He first loved us. His love defines our service with one another.[91]

In the sight of the world, we are indeed Christ's disciple when His love is the one that binds us. In the devil's perception, he knows that when we walk in God's love, he has nothing on us. His fullness fills us up when we walk in God's love.[92]

His love can only be substantiated by the revelation of the Word of God and by the workings of God's Spirit.

Grandeur of Irrelevant Motion

Years ago, while waiting for the traffic light to turn green at the major intersection in Anchorage, Alaska; a man who on his stilled mountain bike at the sidewalk caught my attention. For 20 seconds, without getting his feet off the pedals, his bike stood on one location.

He exhibited a gravity defiance move through his constant balancing motions, then off he goes as soon as the traffic light allowed us to pass through.

Some seemed to have many things going, but what they have is nothing but the grandeur of irrelevant motions. The voice of action is louder than the motions of indecision. Living below or thriving in our potential is an indicator whether we are in pointless motion or in needful action.

Mind you, coining motion as an action is a foolish mistake that we will ever make in life. In perspective, it is much easier to maneuver life when it is moving, because something is going when things are rolling.

Busyness for the things that we do not have the grace to carry out, only procures a back and forth swing like motion. It is flashy, but it never consummates our calling's completion.

Revelation completes God-given assignments when in a corresponding action we crank it up. We go past God's calling unto the Holy Spirit's separation when we heed to God's revealed will. Every revelation requires faith's tangible conviction.

Everything in our existence revolves around with our personal revelation of who God is. The Bible says, they that know their God shall do exploit.[93]   We take advantage of our inheritance in Christ when we engage our knowledge of God into an action of faith. As we realize the calling and purposes that God personally made known to us, by God's grace we take on life challenges victoriously.

Get'r Done is Better Than Later Done

Procrastination mishandles and squanders our God given moments. Our growth potential is delayed when our God's allocated times and seasons for our soul's spiritual development is push aside. When mediocrity settled us down, then we become dull minded with the things of God and stupidities sidetracks our focus.

You see, what positions us to seize our God's defining moments is our engagement with our God ordained pursuits. When we are mindful of the Holy Spirit's direction, our transition into His specified seasons is indispensably timely.

Courage is not lacking when divine truth is encountered. Nonetheless, deferring our faith's engagement towards the revelation that we received from the Holy Spirit, ditches our opportunities on the wayside.

Time is of the essence when it comes to discerning and blazing new open doors. When we run the vision made plain by revelation, a projected result is just a matter of time.

Breaking through unto our divine destiny is the ultimate unfolding of who we authentically are in Christ. Our divine mandate is to bring our whole soul (self) to the entirety of our God intended whole life.

Our life-long divine mandate is to engage ourselves in the battle front - which is the possession of our minds for Christ. God given seasons are designated for specified heavenly mandates and calling. Therefore, any inconsistencies only defer the manifestation of our inheritance in Christ.

It makes sense that each piece of the puzzle that the Holy Spirit and we - the children of God rightly connect onto the board of life is a completed section towards the completed whole.

Yes, we are talking about the suitable action that settling to the finishing point. Even though, expectations are seemingly delayed, waiting on God is all just a part of it. What makes us run the faith race with patience is the joy of the destiny that awaits us.[94]

The growth potentials wired-up in our Divine Nature Attributes-DNA are passion driven by the Spirit of God. Active faith is what differs a commitment from indifference. What tied us up in religious dormancy are apprehensions that keeps on enunciating but lacking in engagements.

Hesitation gets us nowhere. If the faith that we claim is lifeless or inactive, then it deprives our soul of spiritual breakthroughs. Consistent action proves that faith is alive. Growth is the evidence of breakthrough; deficiency shows the lack thereof.

The knowledge that lacks relevance is an exercise in futility. The Holy Spirit enables us to connect dots together in our sphere of influence, such authenticity separates our life as purposeful from mere trending. Christ is the Head, and we are His Body.

The chosen few who were from among many are the rare ones because they're the only people who lovingly apply their belief to their God's receipt of revelation.

What Christ achieved and completed is already ours, but we cannot manifest such inheritance unless our faith corresponded (or agreed) with the Spirit and the Word. All His promises are all yes, we must say Amen (agree) to all of it!

God's momentum builds our monument of greatness. We capture a supernatural event when we yield to do His will. As we kick it up a notch, our seized God-given moment breeds exponential drive once it is ongoing; we must constantly change the size of the growth room to accommodate its ever-increasing opportunities.

You will be surprised to discover that every time Jesus talks about God's intention towards His children; He explicitly tied it up with the word "Go." Go is the first two letters of God and the Gospel. God is always on the go. We missed our divine timing and stale our God-given opportunity when we do not go.

The feet of them that go and preach the Good News are beautiful; they resonate heaven's immensity of glory. Our going with His will confirms the alignment of our soul for His cause.

The Bible is full of testimonies where the Father manifested Himself as the covenant-keeping God to those who in faith acted upon their God-given revelation.[95] Our destiny in Christ unravels the transformation of our soul.

Processing the spiritual invasion of our soul is a life-long commitment. With the revealed Sword of the Holy Spirit at our disposal, it is our responsibility as believers to extend our soul's spiritual territories.

Our soul is the intermediary between the spiritual and physical world. Therefore, our transformed soul opens the flow of heaven on earth.

Spirit, and Soul, and Body

What balances life is our correct perspective and understanding of who we are as a tripartite being. The sequence of our divine order is we are a spirit, we have a soul, and we live in a body. Shuffling this arrangement causes an inconsistent life with the will of God.

Confusing our spirit as our soul and vice versa will make the spiritual growth as an elusive pursuit. Without the fundamental understanding of this subject, we will never have a correct interpretation and application of the scripture, more so to our approaches with God's grace, faith, and God's glory.

Our life in Christ is designed to operate from the inside going out; when we try to live from the outside coming in, then the life that God have in mind for us is unrealizable.

Living from the inside out means having our existence based on God's divine order; that is, our body manifests the essence of our spirit who governs the persona of our soul.

Pursuing our destiny in Christ means, we are passionate to manifest on the outside the work that God already finalized within us.

Yes, essential on how our faith can engage God's purposes are our perception on how our born-again spirit operates, our understanding of what is God's restoration program for our soul, and how we link our living sacrificed flesh to the Holy Spirit's outpouring of His glory.

God who worked inside of us is also the same God who works through us. The work of the Lord did not just start and then get settled within. It is designed to ultimately manifest externally.

The Eternal life that began in our spirit is the essence of God that affects our soul, and eventually manifest in the flesh.

Regarding our spiritual position, there are no more works to offer in satisfying God's expectation. All that Jesus accomplished on the cross and His resurrection is who we now are in Christ; with regards to our inheritance in Christ, He already stamped them with His resounding YES.

However, with respect to our soul's temporal earthly position, we must come into an agreement with what God has already accomplished through Christ. We must say, SO BE IT (AMEN) in my soul oh Lord! Our spirit does not adjust with our soul, On the contrary, our soul must align with who we already are in Christ in our recreated spirit.

Vital Versus Trivial

When the raging bull knows that its real adversary is the matador, will it hit the right target and not waste its time and energy?

By the matador's deceptive flaunting of the cape, the animal was made to believe that it was doing the right thing. Sadly, the animal in his vast strength and potential becomes a spectacle and a sacrifice.

Our real challenges are not worldly conditions and situations that we daily come up against, but it is rather our disposition towards them. Addressing the wrong issues only sets us up for defeat and failure.

Dealing with the right issue decides how we discover the right solution and appropriately spin our circumstances towards our soul's ongoing transformation.

When we focus and engage our hearts on the essential, all obstacles that tries to shrink our momentum to sheer motion will be dished out in the full-scale measure.

We are a spirit that possesses a soul, and we live in a physical body. Reversal of this order is the cause of defeat and bondages among many of God's children. We cannot operate in the flesh trying to spiritualize our soul; such religion will never work.

The reason we keep on encircling the same mountain all our lives is that we tried to exist the other way around (instead of living from the inside out, we try to live from the outside going in).

Attempting to communicate our being into view from outside going in, will only burn us out. We will be blown by exhaustion when we try to believe through presumption. Baseless audacity is a motion that does not come to fruition.

Trying to merit God's approval on what we can externally perform does not accomplish Christ's sanctioned spirituality. By His grace, you are already spiritual on the inside. Therefore, extend it from the inside out. What resonates our being is the life that is coming from our spirit man within.

God's divine order is spirit, soul, and body. What set our body as a living sacrifice for God's service is our transformed soul, and what dispenses spirituality to our soul is our recreated spirit.

The life that proceeded from the inside is the life that manifests our true being in Christ. The life that moves from the outside is a life that exerts living that keeps on trying but never comes to consummation.

We must dismiss the needless and esteem the essential. Our downturn is our busyness over trivial matters. We can only put off the old man by putting on the new man. We can only practically display the defeat of the evil by doing good.[96] We handle wrong stuff correctly when we apply the truth.

I mean for crying out loud, stop fighting sin; focus on being the righteousness of God in Christ our Lord. Quit focusing on non-essentials; use your time to enjoy your life in the presence of God. Instead of stressing yourself about a problem, major on majors, minor on minors, and disregard all inconsequential.

We overcome temptation, test, and trials by seeking first Christ's Lordship and His righteousness. Our failure stems from trying to overcome the devil's curve ball by trying to merit the expected end. Our submission to Christ kingly dominion is what keeps us to be on where we are at in Him.

Jesus is our yesterday, today, and forever. Jesus said, He will never leave you nor forsake you; so, in whatever stage of time you are at, believe that you are in Christ!

The Balance View of Grace

The New Covenant is all God through His man and the plan of God concerns man's redemption through Christ; taking man out of the picture dissipates the medium of expression of the purpose of God. We understand why and what God saved us when we work out the salvation that God already worked inside of us. Prophet Joel said,

> "And it shall come to pass afterward that I will pour out My Spirit on all flesh.
>
> Joel 2:28 NKJV

A renewed mind that offers a physical body as a reasonable worship. A living sacrificed body epitomizes the will of God as good, acceptable, and perfect. On earth, it is God's good pleasure to work through a man who loves Him and who walks in His purpose.

Contradictory, man prides himself on what he can accomplish on his own. Nonetheless, grace is exemplified when we submit our will to do the will of God for the Bible says; God gives more grace to the humble.[97]

Fulfilling God's calling is done by His grace enabling us. It is a far cry from man's fleshly initiated religious fireworks. Self-entitlement has no place in the purposes of God, we cling only to what Christ has done for us. We live under the Holy Spirit's leadership and His revelation of who Christ is within us,

God offered us His grace of salvation; we receive this salvation through faith. God is the giver and we are the receiver. The gift finds its purpose when it is received and enjoyed by the recipient.

The grace of God's salvation is free, and it can only be received and engaged through faith. God's grace initiatives and believer's consistent receptivity of God's grace balances a spiritual stance. Once it is given and received, finding its way of expression is indispensable.

There is nothing more that we need than a balanced belief. However, man's tradition will never balance spirituality, neither human based religious performance. Only the truth equates balance. Only the truth defines true spirituality. Grace has no definition in the absence of truth.[98]

From the very beginning, the Bible portrays the amazing grace of God. In the garden of Eden, before Adam and Eve had the chance of replenishing the earth, God already gave them everything they need. They failed because they tried to establish themselves on their own.

The word mercy in the Old Covenant is the word grace transliterated in the New Covenant. We cannot say that God woke one day and decided to be gracious because it is the New Covenant time! The Father of the heavenly lights does not change like shifting shadows.[99] Jesus is the same yesterday, today, and forever.

The New Covenant is full of believer's example of grace responses towards the undeserving. For example: walking the extra mile, turning the other cheek, loving your enemy, seasoning our speech with grace, forgiving seven times seventy, and so on and so forth.

The principle of grace in the Bible has two sides. First, the eternal solution of God in which God's provision is active, and man is passive. There is absolutely nothing that can qualify a man for God's extended arms of grace. However, once the grace of God engulfed our hearts, such causes us to actively participate with His will. It is God's divine nature (the same grace) that teaches us to engage and escape ungodliness and worldly desires.[100]

The grace of God is both spiritual and practical. Any spirituality in the absence of practicality is just a lofty ideal incapable of blessing the world. Ministry is an outflow of what is real on the inside. God's provision of grace and man's application of grace is what comprises Biblical Christianity.

Spiritually, our heart's adherence to God's grace determines our generosity in every practical thing and every good work. Directing our focus on everything Christ accomplished on the cross shapes the tenacity of our faith.

What is the purpose of having a hang glider if we do not even know how to fly and land it? What is the use of claiming an ownership of a firm belief and when life gives us an opportunity to share it to our detractor, we then shy away and profiled them as; "you're different from us."

Can we honestly assert that we believe in grace and yet we refuse to be gracious to those who failed our expectations? Are we just heavenly minded without earthly goods? The grace of God does not nullify the will of man but strengthen him on the inside with the revelation knowledge. Apostle Paul said,

Chapter 6: Hardwired for Breakthrough

> *...and He died for all, that those who live should live no longer for themselves, but for Him who died for them and rose again.*
>
> *2 Corinthians 5:15 NKJV*

Something divine is bound to manifest when God is operating in our lives. Life's conditions can be an event that triggers a divine encounter when our pursuit is the will of God. The Lord is indeed at work through us when His will is taking place in our lives.

Possessing our minds with the understanding of the life eternal that God has already attributed our spirit with predisposes us to display His will to the whole world.

God gives more grace when we recognize that on our own, we cannot do anything without His guidance and empowerment. Grace is God's side of the ledger; faith is man's recognition of grace and the divine-given ability to receive it.

> *But He gives more grace. Therefore He says: "God resists the proud, But gives grace to the humble." Therefore submit to God. Resist the devil and he will flee from you. Draw near to God and He will draw near to you...*
>
> *James 4:6-8 NKJV*

The grace of God is unrealistic outside our participation with what the Holy Spirit revealed to us. We can misapply and obstruct God's grace by thinking that we can pull things together outside His anointing, revelation, and leadership.

God's grace has no more room to empower us when we try it on our own. Grace living is made possible through the guidance and direction of the Spirit of grace.

Man and God's Plan

We have more to become in our soul than what we less now are. Based on the level of our current condition, aligning our soul to our recreated spirit's class of being is imperative.

God is constantly revealing, and a man of faith is ceaselessly receiving. A transformed soul is a catalyst where God's purposes on earth are practically carried out. Like the pre-fallen Adam, we become fully functional (spirit, soul, and body) when the Spirit of the Lord fuses our recreated spirit into our soul. We usher heaven on earth when our soul is transformed by His glory.[101]

God crowned man with glory and honor when He created him a little lower than Himself – Elohim; then He authorized man (Adam and Eve) to be in charge over the rest of the creation.[102]

The mandate of men and women in Christ is to rule the earth. Jesus - the Second Adam shows us how we can do it. In His 3-1/2 earthly years of ministry, He exemplified to us how to reign in life through the anointing of the Holy Spirit and by the revelation of the Word. We can live out the distinction of our resurrected life in Christ when by His Spirit we live life from the inside out.

Christ is the Spirit, and the Church is His Body. The Church is the evidence and the representation of God's purposes on this planet. We cannot hold our silence anymore in expressing God's praises and honor.

If after considering Christ's revelation and still we chose not to magnify His Name, then rocks will rise in praise in our place instead, and for certain, the earth will travail with shakings. Do we want rocks rising like this? Who in his right mind like earthquakes?

Completing the Man of His Plan

> *And I am certain that God, who began the good work within you, will continue his work until it is finally finished on the day when Christ Jesus returns.*
>
> *Philippians 1:6 NLT*

God is aiming for the manifestation of the fullness of His plan in the Church. We were chosen in Christ to share this spiritual journey. What God initiated within us is also what God the Father is pledged to fulfill.

The Lord can bring our soul in wholeness and the Holy Spirit is the seal that guarantees our soul's completion. He called whom He predestined, He justified whom He called, and He will ultimately glorify whom he justified.[103]

Yes, during our life on earth, God will never leave us nor forsake us until He fulfills His plan and purposes for our lives. God backs up His man who lives according to His plan. As we pursue of His purpose in love, God promised to break us through from every life's challenges.[104]

Our destiny unfolds when out of love we actively take our assigned part in the tapestry of His plan. When His will becomes the epicenter of our existence, we are predisposed to manifest the richness of His life.

Are we being transformed from the inside out or from the external we are being conformed with the system of the world? Change is internal. On the other hand, compromising is allowing the external world to have its influence over us.

Where does our soul's persona takes its form? What fashion our minds? Are we being molded by the worldly system or by the revelation of Christ and His redemption?

When we let the Holy Spirit stands out on the inside and let Him invade our soul with His anointing and revelation, from glory to glory our soul transforms into same image of His glory.

Having God equips us with a sovereign will, confirms the fact that He wants us to employ ourselves for His glory. Was God just filling up spaces when He gave us a physical body and a mind that can reason out, imagine, and think?

Everything God has given us was designed to serve His purpose. Anything that is being said of a man that tries to nullify God's purpose must be scrutinized and rejected. Jesus once said in a parable, "…well done, good and faithful servant." Seriously, can you be faithful towards God without an active participation on your part in endorsing His glory?

How do you think God will be able to complete the good work he began in our lives? God is at work through us when His will is the deciding element of our life's choices.

We carry out things critical to our destiny when we choose His will rather of our own. In every situation, we are ordained to base our responses from the wellspring of eternal life within us. The book of Proverbs said;

> *Keep vigilant watch over your heart; that's where life starts.*
>
> *Proverbs 4:23 MSG*

Bonding our faith with what God heavily invested within our new creation spirits sparks the fuse of our inner man to rise and takes over our outward condition.

By believing God, out of our innermost being we streams rivers of hope giving water. In Christ, we are completely complete within. Our regenerated spirit has full access and claim on everything that our Lord Jesus accomplished on the cross and His resurrection.

What releases us from the restrictions of our natural senses is God's divine flow within our recreated spirit. Such resurrection life will not manifest without the transformation of our soul.

Salvation, Righteousness, and Faith

We traditionally think that the spirit is the one growing spiritually. Is it? God is perfect and an absolute being. Therefore, we cannot claim that the spirit that He regenerated in us is incomplete and inadequate.

God can only give what He has. Therefore, we cannot say that our new creation spirit - where all things are of God, where old things have passed away, and all things become new - is not complete and whole.

Our soul is the one that needs growth. Through the Word and the Spirit, our soul can breakthrough from being dysfunctional unto fully spiritually operational. Our soul's spiritual understanding of the salvation that we received from Christ must come to maturity.

When the breath of life – the spirit - merged into the body of Adam, such divine fusion resulted into Adam becoming a living soul - an inanimate flesh became the expression of a living persona who interacted with his God and his world. How then God restores and matures our soul? The Holy Spirit through Apostle Paul's epistle to Romans gave us a clue.

> *For I am not ashamed of the Gospel of Christ, for it is the power of God to salvation for everyone who believes, for the Jew first and also for the Greek. For in it the righteousness of God is revealed from faith to faith; as it is written, "The just shall live by faith."*
>
> Romans 1:16-17 NKJV

These three words: salvation, righteousness, and faith are extremely vital into the understanding our soul's spiritual growth. However, in laying a groundwork in understanding spiritual breakthrough, using the words salvation and righteousness in synonymous terms is crucial.

These two words meant the life of Christ that He freely provided for us through His cross and His resurrection. Salvation or righteousness consists of our right standing, spiritual position, identity, calling, and destiny in Christ. Nowadays, we cheaply coined the word salvation as our "band aid" for hell, and we never took advantage of this life eternal to the maximum.

Faith: An Insight to our Righteousness in Christ

> *For in it, the righteousness of God is revealed from faith to faith...*
>
> Romans 1:17 NKJV

In the context of Romans 1:15-17, the word faith means a spiritual insight of the righteousness or salvation that we received in Christ. Faith is a spiritual revelation that helps us practically translate our new creation reality to our temporal world.

Faith is what makes the salvation or righteousness practically operational. In the Gospel, God reveals His righteousness from faith to faith. Faith is the lifestyle of a steadfast conviction based on a solid revelation of the Word. Faith personifies the salvation we received from God. Faith is a link that connects Christ's reality to our earthly practicality.

The question is, does the righteousness - the great salvation that God gave us through Christ grow from one stage of the revelation of faith to the next? No! The Righteousness of God - God's Salvation on the inside of us is perfect and absolute. Paul said, "we are complete in Him who is the Head of all principality and power." Through and through, you are the righteousness of God in your recreated spirit.[105]

The one who is spiritually growing is our soul's spiritual understanding of our righteous standing in Christ. Unless our soul grows into such understanding, there is no way we can personify our righteous position in Christ unto our earthly temporal existence. We are mandated by God to rule the earth. Only a living soul in Christ can do that.

We Reign When He Lord Over Us

31...If God be for us, who can be against us?

Romans 8:31 NKJV

The word "for" in this scripture also means "over." This scripture can also be render as, "If God be over us, who can be against us?" We reign when He reign over us. God over you are equal to the manifestation of your ultimate victory; that is your divine mathematical expression.

Man, outside God's greatness is naked and exposed to the elements of spiritual wickedness. Our soul streaming in harmony with God's divine intention, set us up to God's divine flow. God never abandon His purpose for man. Settling in His will gives us the ringside view on how God turn anything the devil throws at us for our advantage.[106]

When David faced Goliath, it was just him and God over him. When Jesus defeated the death on the cross, it was just Him and the Father's will over Him. The cost of dying to pride and seeking the preeminence of His Kingdom is imperative to our realization of the great salvation that God has given us.

We only find freedom in the place where the Spirit of God reigns.[107] Freedom is not an autonomy where we have self-determination in everything we do. Living independently from God ensures disaster at the end.

When we allow Jesus to be the King and Lord over our lives, we reign in life as kings and rule over the worldly system as lords. The measure of Christ's grace that He gifted and anointed us will find its expression in our lives when Christ by His Spirit is the One reigning over us. We are all designed to see and engage our identity in Christ. God over you resonate the ultimate statement of you.

Through the new birth, Jesus by His Spirit came to indwell us. With Him, everything that He accomplished on the cross and everything He gained from His resurrection came along. Such life eternal that we have in Christ from within must sequentially go out to our soul and outwardly manifest to our body.

The life that we have now in Christ is full of God's righteousness (Jesus' right standing with the Father). This kind of life must break out from the inside out.

CHAPTER SEVEN
Breaking through the Obvious
We realized His promise when we see as God sees

Positioning Yourself to See

> *Moreover the word of the Lord came to me, saying, "Jeremiah, what do you see?" And I said, "I see a branch of an almond tree." Then the Lord said to me, "You have seen well, for I am ready to perform My word."*
>
> Jeremiah 1:11-12 NKJV

Whenever the Lord said, 'see' or 'behold' in the Scripture, this indicates of His invitation to align our hearts with the way He sees things. His passion penetrates our natural existence through the revelation of His plan and His purposes; such is the moment where faith is grabbing ahold of the heartbeat of the Lord. We are hopelessly blind without His eyes.

Seeing the way God perceives things, position our soul's understanding into receiving what He promised to perform. Hearing the voice of the Lord or seeing His intention per se, shifts us to a place where He can explicitly manifest Himself through us on the earth.[108] In Christ, we can access a level of relationship with God the Father where we see things eye to eye with Him.

Until we recognize the futility of our physical eyes' concerning God's invisibility, engaging ourselves with His plan and purposes is a wavelength beyond our natural grasp. Letting the Holy Spirit have His way is what engages our whole being to live out God's will.

In our walk with God, we must look past the obvious and seize what the Holy Spirit is spontaneously revealing from our spirit into our minds. Often, we miss these instructive revelations as previewed messages for pending events as we let the material world dominates our thought life. Take this to heart, trying to run a spiritual operation through presumptive notions will get us drown if we try to walk on water.

Unsettled emotions and the absence of inner peace are direct results of our non-participation with His will. Our engagement in the realm of God comes about when we operate within the framework of our spirituality in Christ. We spiritually navigate life through faith and not by sight.

Faith is the capacity to see things beyond what our physical eyes cannot. Visually challenging aspects of life can quickly throw us off when we try to run spirituality based on our natural ability; on our own, we are at the mercy of our natural conditions.

In regards with our negative external circumstance, the Lord Jesus Christ told us in the Gospel; "…take no thought SAYING."[109] We may not fully apprehend this fact, but our mouth is a gate of our spirituality in this world. Faith is the only way we can relate with the invisible God while living in the visible world.

We cannot formulate who God is by our logic and wild imaginations. Sensationalizing our dealing with life's circumstance through religious articulation, will not do us any good. Time will tell if our claimed "thus saith the Lord expressions" was a revelation or "wish- on" coined as a spiritual vision.

During challenging situations, instead of pseudo-spiritualizing our natural circumstances, we should pray and give thanks to God. When we flow in faith, we are opening ourselves into the ability of seeing things from God's perspective.

When by faith we uncluttered our minds for God, the Holy Spirit can quicken our mortal bodies in a state where He can even use our natural senses to discern good and evil. Remember Apostle Paul said, "…our members can be an instrument of righteousness."[110]

God is convincingly convincing. Conviction is our spiritual navigational device amidst the unknown challenging terrain that we are trekking. Conviction is faith's inward eye and ear.

A conviction can apprehend unrealized goals and persuades us of its reality in the here and now. We are not ready for what is ahead until from the inside we perceived the revelation of the Spirit. Capturing God-given vision provides us a solid sustaining ground for life. Flowing with what God wants us to walk on provides us a platform where we see things beyond our natural eyes. What limits us is our self-made boxes, where we insist God to fit Himself in.

What hinders us is not the intimidation of the foreseen and the unforeseen future events. What defines us is not what we lack in the natural. What truly identify us is who we are in Christ. When from the inside, we get ahold of His greatness, then demonstrating His magnitude into the open is just a given. When we are drawing our perspective from the Holy Spirit's inward conviction; we are always dead centered with God's divine order. The book of Proverbs says, "Knowing what right is like deep water in the heart; a wise person draws from the well within."[111]

Growth is Secured Where God Planted Us

Growth is part of God's plan. Apart from Christ, our soul will not grow in understanding who we are in Him. We can only find the fullness of what God has cut for us in the place where He planted us.

Discovering such a position is essential for our growth and spiritual breakthrough. Such is the place where bearing fruit and stirring up of gifts flows typically supernatural. Sadly, some parts of the Body of Christ seek spiritual advancements while they swim like a fish out of the water or trying to be established into an environment that they do not really belong.

God's prophetic vision takes us to our calling's completion. The book of Proverbs says, "…without a prophetic vision, people will purposelessly roam around."[112]

We have access to spiritual perceptivity in the place where God has planted us. Your eyes can see because it is rightfully connected. Your specified part in the Body of Christ is liberating and a place where God's measured of anointing on your life fully flows.

Let Go of your Stick

To conduct the chimp's emotional study, a scientist monitors the animal being hold inside a well-lit concrete room. Right away, a familiar scent caught the animal's attention and he came to investigate what was inside the canister bolted in the middle of the chamber. However, the container's opening was not wide enough for his forearm to go all the way through and retrieve his favorite food at the bottom of the metal jar.

The chimp screams and ran around to vent his frustration; in the process, he found a wooden stick. The chimp grabbed and used it as a tool to try and get the treat out. To its dismay however, though the chimp could move its choice food inside the canister with its new-found device, the animal is still unable to extract the treat out of the cylinder.

Along the way, the chimp got extremely irritated as it wanted to take its hand out of the canister, but the animal trapped its own hand by not letting the stick go. Out of desperation, the animal pounded its head many times against the concrete wall and eventually mortally injured itself.

The chimp's greediness of the stick - his perceived hope to secure his desired treat – downplayed its opportunity to discover the hidden button that tilts the canister. So, by letting his emotion to do the thinking and decision for himself, the animal got out of control and lost its purpose.

In the same way, we are trapped when we are caught off guard in the things that we attached ourselves emotionally. Our soul deteriorates when we keep on settling for the things that are less valuable than what we were ordained by God to pursue.

We are designed to seek and be founded on what Christ has gained for us on the cross and His resurrection. On every front, the visible temporal comfort of the natural things will always hinder us from perceiving our soul's spiritual breakthrough. Therefore, letting go of our obvious limitations and trading it for faith's ventures of the invisible is essential. Let go of the trivial and let God be your breakthrough door opener.

Breaching the External

The 'thinking outside the box' slogan has been around for decades and such catchphrase urges us go past the norm and reflect beyond the ordinary.

What an impressive motivational punchline! Nonetheless, obliterating the box itself is more viable option because such eradication leaves no room to patronize ourselves to mediocrity.

A box is a hollow container with four solid sides and a top and a bottom covering. What boxed you in, contains you! To make the story short, it sorts you out with its limited and average description of yourself.

Naturally, we are within the limitation of time, space, and physical senses; that is, the known material world boxed us up within its defined limitation. Our natural restrictions impose controlled points of reference and regulates our would-be action to just restricted operation.

What then is the box that limits you from growing? What is the box that restrains you from seeing and realizing God's unseen realities for your life? What is the box that instigates a lifestyle of commonplace?

Righteousness, peace, and joy: which is the essence of God's Kingdom will remain inaccessible when we settle to idle ourselves within our human possibilities. Breaking out from these limiting boxes can only be done through Holy Spirit's guidance and direction.

Life would be ridiculously awful if we resigned ourselves to our natural restrictions. If we allow our natural senses imposed what will our condition be, that will be it for us; there is nothing more but all is less.

What involves in breaking these restraining boxes is us coming into the realization of the platform where which we can transcend our natural circumstance into grasping God's divine intention.

To break through from these boxes, we must go past the three-dimensional world and begin tapping the realm of God – which is our life in Christ in the fourth dimension.

Experiencing our soul's spiritual breakthrough is an outcome of admission of two things. First, you are inside a restricted box, and secondly, you need Jesus' revelation to break you free from these boxes.

The knowledge of our problems will not liberate us from its influence. What takes care of the perceived restrictions is the solution or the answer if you will. Light is the answer to darkness. Christ and all that He did for us is the only solution. He is the weapon of our warfare that is mighty than all carnal complications combined. [113]

Seeing His children in the full manifestation of their sonship is the Father's good pleasure. Bringing our divine ordained capacity to its maximum expression is the accommodation that God is more than willing and able to perform.

It is His dream that our soul should come to our fullness in Christ. Nevertheless, we can only realize such purpose when we walk from the inside out and not from the life that is from the outside going in.

Just like on flying kites, we cannot do it without the wind. Even so, we cannot comprehend our destiny in Christ without the operation of the Spirit and the revelation of the Word.

We simultaneously exist in two worlds: spiritual and natural. As much as we need to satisfy our external existence with natural bread, our priority is to satisfy our soul's spiritual need with God's spoken Word. Jesus said, "…man shall not live by bread ALONE, but by every word that proceeds out of the mouth of God…"[114]

We are spirits within a physical body. If what we only allow to define us are what natural things can classify us, then we will never come to realize our true being and fulfill our divine destiny in Christ. There is more to life than external things. Every time we tap into the realm of the Spirit, our God given purpose is absorbing our soul – mind, emotion, and will.

Kingdom living has eternal consequence, and we can initialize it from within. We must see things first through our inward eyes and grasped God-given vision from the wellspring of God's Spirit within. Basing our response from the inside is the way to negate and pull down external carnal sentiments.

Life is not because the way things are. The way things turned out is decided by the way we are. The manner we see ourselves on the inside will always affect the way we respond and react to every given life's opportunity.

We see things through our way of thinking. Only the reborn spirit can see the Kingdom of God. Therefore, for us to see what God is in the process of leaking His glory from His throne releases our soul to manifest His will on earth.

A mind dominated by the flesh is a carnal mind. A mind governed by the Spirit and the revealed Word is a mind that manifests the life of God and His divine order - His peace.

A negative person constantly finds a way to speak up his carnal mind simply because external things is what captivates his soul. Therefore, He does not mind calling out the wrongs on everything and everyone.

External impressions are always the basis of the pessimist's mind. Once the skeptic's worldly perceived solutions are exhausted, it cannot move forward to discover a lasting solution.

Nonetheless, life should always start from within and not from without. A carnal mind cannot fathom God's providence because it can only be seen in faith; such goes beyond what man can see with his natural eyes.

Our inward fortitude decides our outward disposition. Getting a hold of His purpose in the spirit of meekness is vital. Our frame of mind must be regulated by a spiritual perceptivity rather than by natural senses. Internal condition regulates external expression.

Manifestations of God's goodness cannot be otherwise but the real thing when our inward potentials in Christ seized in faith.

Chapter 7: Breaking through the Obvious

Trigger the Tigger

> *Keep your heart with all diligence, for out of it spring the issues of life.*
>
> *Proverbs 4:23 NKJV*

Our soul's carnal propensity is constantly fed by external impressions. What saturates our hearts are what we ooze out amidst life's pressures.

Sentiments that overwhelm our hearts will find their form of expression through words, gestures, and action. Life does not commence from the outside; it begins from the inside.

There is an internal life and an external life. We reduce our existence as of the animal world when we adhere to the latter. A body without a spirit is dead. The spirit is the essence of the physical life.

The spiritual must be the pivotal influence or the principle of the external. One's spirituality in Christ must be the core value of his external reality and not the other around.

We draw life from God's well of salvation and not from our own self-centered negotiation. We issue our life's greatest edition when we guard our focus from the inside.[115]

The revealed Word of God (Christ and His Redemption) is the only one that can safeguard our hearts. David said, "your word have I hid in my heart that I may not sin against you."[116] The Word of God is our window to the realm of God.

Keeping His Word in our hearts is like having a set of eyes that has a higher viewing platform of what life should be. Seeing from God's point of view enables us to assess life with hope, confidence, and joy despite the pressure of external limitations.

The way God sees us in our earthly existence is from the perspective of His Word. If the Word of God says, "…we can do all things through Christ," then that should settle it. The revealed Word of God is a platform where we can approach life.

When we keep God's revelation in our hearts, then the revealed Word from within will keep us from anything that stands in our way.[117] We can only understand God with our spirit. The Lord speaks to our spirit. He relates to us internally. What He deals with us on the inside is what we can extend though us on the outside.

The way we live is a result of the way we inwardly see ourselves. There will always be a restriction when we try to engage life from the external influence. We are a spirit that possesses a soul, and we live in a physical body. Therefore, we must be vigilant on where we soak our hearts consistency; for out of the inward recession of our being, we spring forth life's circulations. When you know that He lives in you, you will let Him live through you.

Breaking Out from our External Religiosity

Is it faith or self-squeezed will of man's tradition? Religion hides its spiritual nakedness through external performances; The fear of man is what heavily drives and motivates religion. God is on the outside looking in when we try to merit spirituality on our natural strength. We cease to operate as God's conduit of His divine flow when we esteem our tradition higher than our Lord Almighty.

Religion practices openly, but it often filled with inward dissatisfaction. It mistakenly presumes that it advances itself spiritually by external initiative, but the more it practices its tradition, the more it diminishes itself to just ritualistic expression. Paul the Apostle describe it as;

Chapter 7: Breaking through the Obvious

> *...having a form of godliness but denying its power.*
> *And from such people turn away!*
>
> 2 Timothy 3:5 NKJV

Religion makes self its focal point and elevates own will above God's will. Religion's servitude towards God is always per its external notion, and it is far from God's guidance and Holy Spirit's leadership. We start building our self-instituted altar to reach heavens when we-the church intentionally shuns the power and the influence of the Holy Spirit. Religion is none other but a self-made perceived spiritual institution.

For the length of two months back in 2013, I had an opportunity to pastor a church in California where 70% of its parishioner belongs to one family. There was an incident when out of financial stress, a member of the church's worship team compromised himself back to the world doing the drug thing; I advised him not to play as part of the church disciplinary action.

He disproved me and told me that no pastor or nobody could dictate what he can and cannot do inside the church. He called his sister who happened to be the chairperson of the church's board; thus, the sister rebuked me and told me that I judged his brother for not having a clear discernment of her brother's heart condition. I responded, "Yes I may not completely understand what your brother's heart's condition is, but what he exactly did is enough to bar him from involving in the worship team."

My pastoral decision was more of telling this local church that God mean business when it comes to worship. Therefore, shunning the said brother's involvement to church's worship was more of protecting him. For the scripture says; "…you shall not tempt the Lord your God."[118]

A week later, I sent text messages to every member of the board who was at that time having a meeting behind my back; I told them; "I am quitting the pastorate. I cannot be in this church that is run by men." It is sad to see that the said church reduced to a family enterprise, having the appearance of Christianity, but ignoring the revealed will of God.

Self is the basis behind every religious operation. It tries to fulfill God's commandments with all its squeezed self-willed power. Even in the matter of ministerial service, religion obscures the Holy Spirit's ministry as it orientates on the strength of self-willed tradition.

Religion works from without, but the Kingdom of God operates from within. Spiritual breakthrough commenced from the inside and not through man's external performance. For the church to breakthrough from religious bondage unto the life of grace, God's eternal life must be internally recognized as real time reality within our spirit; all we must do is to flow through it.

In the Kingdom of God, we have the Holy Spirit who can take us to places where we have never been before and propels us to experience Kingdom's inheritance.

The Holy Spirit is our helper; He can enable us to speak God's creativity into existence. Occasion point, when we are speaking in tongues from our spirits, we let God speak into existence the mysteries of His Kingdom.

We may be zealous and religiously on fire, but if the fire of the Holy Spirit is not the one that is burning us, we will always end up physically and mentally exhausted. The burning bush that Moses saw atop Mount Sinai was profusely burning, but it is not getting incinerated because the presence of God Almighty is the One consuming the bush. God's relationship with us and us with Him is the divine connection that keeps the fire of the Spirit going.

Any performance outside God's relationship is just a bone-dry religion. Performance is not able to replace the commendation of the presence of God because they are all commenced by grace. Paul said, "I am what I am by the grace of God."[119]

Let us step up to the plate of grace because we are God's burning bushes for this generation. Spirituality in the absence of the presence of God is a bone-dry religion, and it is a ridiculous, tedious proposition. Our church services must pass the traditional reading and narration of biblical stories but void of supernatural realities.

CHAPTER EIGHT
Breakthrough Transcends Time
Breakthrough affects the past, the future, and the present

The Divine Commodity of Time

The Lord has totally grasped the shutting down the whole shebang of time even way before it initially gets off the ground. There is no time deviation with God. Each references of time are all in the same plane with Him.

To accommodate man however, the Lord aggregated the time by taking a portion of eternity and sectioned it in the past, the present, and the future. Yes, time marks the beginning, the in between, and the ending.

In its duration, time is inadequate to describe who God is. The Creator is beyond what man can stretch in a measure. The entire boundary of time cannot grasp who God is; He, on the other hand, overwhelms time.

Everything within time is definable by man, and yet God's eternal realm is beyond what human can articulate in words. God holds time's duration, and the Lord's providence is what and where the value of time relies on.

Time is a divine commodity that we expense in carrying out God's purpose in our lives. By using His sectioned time as our point of reference, we suitably connect with our God's master plan.

When we view time as a gift from God, it helps us appreciate it as an element wherein we can offer our lives as a reasonable worship. Stepping into the Lord's glorious acceleration is viably possible when we understand how we can use time in pursuit of His purpose.

When we are in the will of God, time is on our side. Yes, doing the will of God is how we can make the best use of time. God designed time to work for us, and He did not devise it to work against us. However, the tyranny of time will restrict us whenever we brushed aside the will of the Father.

Within our life's period, God has allotted us His grace to increase our soul's spirituality. God uses the time to deal with us, and we use time to serve Him. As we spend our time meditating and interacting with the Holy Spirit concerning God's precious promises, Christ by His grace saturates our soul with His divine nature.[120]

We use time as an opportunity to engage our identity in Christ. It is what the Lord has permitted us to have during our earthly tenure. If God did not provide the time, then there will be no way for us to participate with God's eternal purpose while we are still on earth.

The process in which time is used to carry out God's will be nothing short of; God collaborating with men in occupying this world with the gospel until He comes. Our time on earth serves as a stage wherein we share to the world whatever God the Father has given us in Christ.

We will come to the fullness of our purpose when the Perfect comes. By then, we will no longer then speak, understand, and act like a child, for we shall know just as we are also known.[121] However, until God's realm of eternity have not swallowed up our world of the temporary, we are restrained within the bounds of the in-part knowledge of the eternal.

Despite the restriction of time's framework, however, Christ's supply of grace sets us up with God's defining moments. God the Father provides us with His "Kairos" moment[122] while we are still in our earthly existence.

He regularly breaks us through from our natural limitations unto His temporary (in-part) shared tremendous ability. By the Holy Spirit's revelation, we crack God's perfect moments and experience the manifested flow of His eternal plan. Experiencing His signs and His wonders are occasions of His defining moments with man.

When by way of His revelation we glimpsed through His eyes and participates with His will, the Holy Spirit all at once affects our soul's past, present, and future.

When we flow in God's eternity, the Holy Spirit redeem the time that we've lost in the past, flooded our present existence with Christ's resurrection life, and forged our future with the realization of our soul's divine destiny in Christ.

The Immateriality of the Past

If the future that God is showing us is what makes life buds with hope, then why waste time focusing on irrelevant past? Despite our obsession of cherishing our memories, we cannot hold onto our pasts any longer because they're no longer exist where we are currently at; they're neither here nor there.

What past has left for us to linger in the present are just memories. If I tell you; "I wish, we can go back to where we were at, five years ago, then everything will be all right and dandy. Right?" Wrong! Such sentimental statement may seem sympathetic, but it is just a non-relevant wished-on verbiage.

Can we still grab something that is no longer there anymore? Nevertheless, a lot of us are still stuck on where we have been, and we are getting further behind with God's present laid opportunities.

The Past is past; we cannot do anything about it. Exhausting time in trying to alter an irreversible past is a wasted effort. Come on now; our soul's spiritual drawbacks mostly stemmed from letting our emotions do the scrutiny of our past.

When we allow our emotion sorts out our past life's condition, we tend to lose control, become impulsive, judgmental, and discouraged. If we are emotionally attached with our past's failures, it will not be easy to give it up. Our emotion is not designed to process thoughts and evaluate things.

Moving on is not in the vocabulary of the one who is unwilling to let go. Allowing the painful memory of the past is the reason why the pursuit of forgiveness is difficult. When we are still hanging on things that we already should have been given up, it is tough to let go.

They were painful things that we experienced in the past. Nobody can deny the it, but it does not mean that we are it and we're all done for good.

Seriously, you are not yet perfect in your body and your soul, so do not be hard on yourself. Isn't it funny as imperfect as we are and yet we have a hard time handling our failures?

If a perfect God has forgiven and accepted us, then who are we – an imperfect somebody – so unwilling to forgive and accept ourselves? For us, Christ rose from the dead and in Him we have hope.

God's grace of forgiveness has already covered us up from the beginning, in between, and the end. Only the claim of self's ownership of the past obstructs our heart from understanding that Jesus' blood has wiped our past and nothing on our own where we can satisfy to atone.

After the fall of Adam and Eve, restoration becomes God's first order of business. God specializes in turning life out for the best despite its messes.

The time that we waste in the past is redeemable when we are: in the will of God, continuously getting filled with the Holy Spirit, and enjoying God's presence in the present.[123]

Job of old lost everything he had, but when he shuns from self-pity, complaining, and blaming God for his painful experiences, and began praying for his friends, God redeemed the time that he lost and restored him back twice as much.

The Lord's forgiveness is a matter of redemption and not of condemnation; His love is a substance of restoration and not of destruction. So, stop focusing on the worst, the bad, and the ugly. By faith, start converging with the power and the virtue of Jesus' blood. The blood of the Lamb is eternally saying to us; "we're all acquitted from the stains and the pain of our past sin.

Still Polishing the Chain of Your Past?

Living in the past blurs our present perception, it predisposes us to get easily threatened and intimidated. Such mindset is likening to a frightened ostrich, we bury our heads in the ground and leaving our current lives exposed to the debilitating effects of self-rejection.

Driven with past regrets is a preoccupation of past disappointments that sets us up to mental fatigue; never we can ever reconcile ourselves with reality by recurrently concocting an imagination of making things right with regards to our past mistakes. Our moments dissipate in an aimless and wasteful living when we desperately try to recapture and modify our unalterable past. The past is no longer here with us in the present.

There has nothing exquisite about polishing up the chain of bondage that we were once shackled. We decisively become unfaithful steward of our time when we are still in denial of something that happened in our past.

Why waste time sheltering our setbacks when now God got our back through Jesus' redemptive act. It is rather pointless to direct our life to something already unreal in the present.

The Past is no longer real, but Jesus is! We miss our moments with God in the here and now when we are not employing our energy and creativity to our current tides of life.

You can no longer change your past, but you can always have a better perspective on how you can look at your past in the present. Do not negate yourself of God's blessings; come to the grip of the reality of God's Word and begin to use your imagination in seeing yourself from God's point of view – you are already forgiven and accepted in the beloved!

Your Past has No Future

Life is utterly simple; people are the ones who complicate it. Life goes on at the present; our past is behind our back, and ahead of us is where we aim our future at. Life is all about going forward.

When God put our eyes on our face and not at the back of our heads, He is not just filling up spaces; He is just telling us that unlocking new doors for new things are all in front of us.

We are currently in the now, past is gone, and our future is coming. Our missed past's opportunities pale in comparison to the hope that God reserved for us in the future. Your past has no future.

Your past cannot dictate from where God wants you to go. Regarding your destiny in Christ, your past has no determination towards its fulfillment. Your destiny is God-given, and it never changes regardless of your experience. His gifts and calling are irrevocable.

If for the most part, our consciousness concentrates on reliving our past - we are partly there and partly elsewhere in the present, then giving our all-time best in our current life is nothing but problematic and dysfunctional.

Stalemate is not a promising position because you are stuck in between immobility and futility. Living in the past deprives us of engaging our identity in Christ in the present, and it drains out our future destiny sensitive expectations. It is like wearing spiritual sunglasses with lenses tinted by the past; it affects our present outlook of life.

We become foolish when we allow our past runs our present life. Nonetheless, we can turn our past into a suitable insight for the future when we let the Holy Spirit supplies us with the mind of Christ in the present. By doing so, it enables us not to repeat our past mistakes but wisely use it to guide people who are presently in the same predicament as we were before.

We lose our focus when our minds and emotions are wandering around. However, committing ourselves to God's present revelation gets us quicker to our soul's future destiny but reliving our past delays it.

God's time is always now. He is always ready, but the unrenewed condition of our mind slows us down. He waits patiently for the time where we will come to the awareness of our true being in Christ.

Double Trouble

Living in the past while you are in the present is living with two attentions at a time. Doublemindedness means double soul; it is an existence trapped between two opposing thoughts and two conflicting emotions.

Going in two directions accomplishes nothing; being stuck in between gets us nowhere. Having two motivations only causes disorientation and instability. We lose our focus when our minds and emotions are wandering between our past, present, and future. The Bible says, "Love the Lord your God with all your heart and with all your soul and with your entire mind."[124]

Our present relationship with God the Father is entirely through Jesus or nothing at all. We cannot love Him with some or most of our heart. Our life span is our earthly existence; let us use it wholly for His glory.

Physically present but mentally absent is an expression of someone who is partially current, but somewhat not all there. Some women complained about their husband being with them physically, but not all there with them mentally and emotionally.

The Lord is the Great I AM not the great "I was," nor the great "I will be." He can give us His all because, in the present, all that He is, is all available to us. We can receive His respective measured fullness for our specified time and season when we wholly tuned in with Him in faith.

Our soul's breakthrough in the present fills the gap between the past and the future. God's present revelation of His Christ and His purpose is our link between our earthly reality and heaven's connectivity.

The Old Cannot Handle the New

In 1993, the Marcos government proposed plan for Tenement Housing for people of Smokey Mountain was built under the presidency of Fidel Ramos. The housing project was to benefit people who made their living from scavenging stuff through disposed garbage on the Smokey Mountain.[125]

When I went back to Manila from New York in 1998; I passed by the said housing project and saw that the once well-regarded structures looked so dreadful and filthy. Regardless of the government's effort to alter their lifestyle, the settled image of garbage of Smokey Mountain deep within their hearts found its way to unfold itself in their external lives.

Left to its own, unbroken strongholds that formed our disposition goes with us regardless of the change in residence and life's status. Until we consider and receives fully what Christ's blood has done with our former life, glitches of the past in our present life will always crop itself up and will try to sabotage our potential.

Indeed, our heart's condition determines our external situation. Ultimately, our lives will be in a constant spin if we do not pursue our soul's spiritual transformation in the present. Breakthrough is breaking the restriction of the past to get us through to the expansion of the future.

What Deals the Old is the New

New things do not go well with old stuff. No one wants to dip their freshly cook fries into an old and spoiled sauce. Do you? Of course not!

There will be no breakthrough without disconnecting from the past. Maturity is very unlikely if we keep allowing past's unresolved issues constantly barrage our present engagement in life.

How can we then effectively transition to a new season and break through from an old condition? Spiritual breakthrough is not feasible with an old life.

The only way we can give up the old is to wholeheartedly believe and welcome the new things of Christ that we already have within our spirits. Christ is the fresh anointing within our spirit that can take care of residues of the old man in our soul. Apostle Paul said,

> *that you put off, concerning your former conduct, the old man which grows corrupt according to the deceitful lusts, and be renewed in the spirit of your mind, and that you put on the new man which was created according to God, in true righteousness and holiness.*
>
> *Ephesians 4:22-24 NKJV*

Buried in the graveyard of olden days is our former life; every now and then we tend to resurrect them as zombies apt to chase us and bit us to the end of contaminating our sentiment with guilt and regrets. We may claim that we have a futuristic goal, but our claimed ownership of the past is what grips us in a deadlock position.

Old wineskin cannot contain the new wine of the Holy Spirit. Hosting God's anointing with a life that embodies the past will inevitably waste the divine purpose attached to our lives. The past cannot handle the present nor the future. We cannot have the new things of God and old life mixed up.

Breaking through our life's specific Red Sea season is imperative to the actual manifestation of our relevant God's Promised Land. The old system of Egypt must be broken down from our soul for us to perceive and capture what is waiting for us on the other side. Where our focus is set decides what we spread around.

The new things must flow so that the old should go. Brokenness is essential in renewing the hard and unfruitful ground of the soul. What breaks the old is the new things in Christ! What overcome the evil is the good! What let go of the past is Christ's new life within us. Do not hold back! Lift your sails and catch the newness of God's wind of breakthrough.

Living with the Anxiety of the Future

Jesus asked His disciples a probing question; "Can all your worries add a single moment to your life?"[126] We cannot! Anxieties of the future are robbing us of our moments of creativity and short-circuiting our present appreciation of life's definition.

When present life is not appreciated, its potential is not seized. Jesus furthermore said, "…let the future worry about itself;" So why worry about the future when our handle for life is available for us right now in Christ?

What depletes our energy and triggers nauseated stomach is the worries of the future's respective uncertainties. Most of our overweight problems are from our eating habits that is triggered by anxiety. We mismanage our lifetime through fear and confusion, a mindset of angsts only sanction pointless outlook of life. Ironically, what sets up the life's trajectory into the future are the things that we can run through Christ in the present.

Have you ever wondered why the past and the future sandwiches us in between? Yesterday and tomorrow always sandwiched today. This perpetual condition presents us an opportunity to choose what would make our soul's identity sensible.

We do not base our current existence on the future nor with our past. Jesus is our beginning, our present, and our ending. He is the same yesterday, today and forever.

What we look forward to the future is Him and He is what in the past (His cross and His resurrection) we based our present life with. Jesus and all that He gained for us on the cross, resurrection, and ascension to heaven's thrones is all that we need in life – past, present, and future.

When the future challenges come up current, we do not need to worry because His blessings will show up as supplementary when we make Him our priority. We rule and reign over the natural life when Jesus rules and reigns over our soul's spiritual life.

When we seek the priority of His Lordship and His righteousness (not ours but His), we can rest assured that even when the past and the anxiety of the future pops their ugly head up, God's provision will be there to seek and find us.

As King Jesus reigns over us and His righteousness is the disposition that establishes our hearts, the Father will see to it that we will embody His blessings in every facet of our lives.

> *Be careful for nothing; but in everything by prayer and supplication with thanksgiving let your requests be made known unto God.*
>
> *Philippians 4:6 KJV*

Regardless how big inevitabilities seemingly looms in the future, Paul by the Holy Spirit is telling us, do not worry about those conditions; they are nothing compared to God's faithfulness. Apostle Paul said of them; "…be careful for NOTHING…"

God is telling us not to waste our time for nothing. Instead of worrying about such goose eggs, we must break our way through by unleashing God's power in prayers, supplications, thanksgiving, and bold declaration of what God wants us done on earth as it is in His Heaven.

When we seek to enjoy the company of the Lord and take pleasure in His presence, God will shift our hearts to settle for His best intention.

Life in all its reality is in the present, missing the present is missing the celebration of life's definition. Today, you have the choice to unwrap your present.

Living Where Reality is Taking Place

When the past was current, it was all entirely now. As the future arrives, it will be unequivocally now. Now is constant. Now is eternal.

God, the Father, is not stuck in the past nor restricted in the future, He is presently willing and able to help us where we are at - in the here and now.

In Christ, the great I AM fashioned our spirit with the capacity to release who He is on where we currently at.

Faith is our God-given ability that connects our conceivable temporary with His eternity.

Faith – A Present Spiritual Lifestyle to Live By

Faith empowers us to perceive God's invisibility amidst contradictions in our current visible circumstance. Faith is our present spiritual currency that connects us with the eternal God.

It pleases the Father, when by faith we unite with Him in the now. Faith links heaven up with our present earthly life. Faith enables us to walk with God in the now. Faith is walking on the Word of God – our window into the realm of God in the here and now.

Faith is living currently in the spirit and living in the past is walking in the flesh. When we walk by faith, we break the old system of walking by sight that is so ingrained in our old mindset; we break through from the bondage of carnal limitation unto the freedom of living under the law of the Spirit of life.

God sticks with His original plan regardless of what went down the line in human history. If the Almighty Father wanted Adam to have divine authority from the very beginning; how much more now to those who are already in Christ.

When God sent His Son Jesus, the Father showed us through His Son's example on how the earth can be reigned over. As an illustration point, amid the storm, Jesus spoke of God's divine order by saying; "Quiet! Be still!" Instead of analyzing the problem, He spoke of the solution during the difficulty.

Traditional and religious mindset self-patronizes us in settling on climbing life's spiritual mountains. The truth of the matter is Jesus climbed that mountain with the cross on His back.

In Christ, we are not supposed to scale a mountain of challenges; we are ordained by God to command the mountains and direct them to remove itself and be tossed into the sea.

We brought in the present what we have learned in the past, and we set the platform of the future by believing God in the present. We cannot downplay and disregard the past. How we deal with them in the present through the grace of God, decides what future holds for us.

How we relate with our past in the present can be our thrust unto our leaping forward, or it can plunge to our soul's downsizing. Living the reality of life means living life in the here and now because we can only find real life in the present.

The cross and the resurrection of Jesus is the only past that is worthy of our remembrance. Our Lord Jesus instituted the Lord Supper so that we can commemorate His divine redemption for humanity as often as we can. The cross of our Lord Jesus is our sole divine spiritual history. Christ's cross and resurrection is the divine past that assures victory

Every step that we tread on this current stream of life must set its pace on what our soul can become in Christ. If we do not make use of our time, we will run out of it and the next thing we know, our opportunities are laid waste by the wayside.

What presently disengages us to God's ability that is availably residing within us, is procrastination. A mediocre suspends his engagement until he deemed everything is suitable to his demands.

As opportunity permits, we do not wait for our break; by God's revelation, our faith can break out from the thing that is limiting us. We must aggressively storm heaven with violent faith and claim what rightfully belongs to us in Christ.

Problem breeds curiosity for solutions when we are divinely guided to ask the right question. The Bible says, "…the Holy Spirit will teach us in all things…" Therefore, let us not cease to seek until with His revelation and His divine intervention manifests God's solution for our current condition.

Life is current, and we can only apprehend it in the now. Past adversities have been long gone, and future testing is not yet. Nonetheless, God said; "Behold, now is the accepted time; behold, now is the day of salvation."

Now is your divine opportunity; your faith in God's Word enables you to seize what God promised you in the now. The Lord honored this moment for you; today you can grab ahold of it.

Today is a gift from God. It is a present waiting to be unwrapped; enjoy it and use it for God's greater glory. Today is the day that the Lord has made; rejoice for your Creator is smiling at you in full delight.

Your life is all it is because of what Christ has accomplished for you on the cross and in His resurrection. In Christ, God's countenance is beaming with favor and approval over you. Today is the good day for your soul to breakthrough.

CHAPTER NINE
The Catalyst for Breakthrough
God's grace shaped our past and forged our future

Forgiveness: Our God-given Restart Button

On one weekend, I casually watched my youngest son Ezekiel played a tricky but highly competitive military operation video game. He failed on numerous tries to complete the game's combat campaigns.

To say the least, what slapped him repeatedly is the "game over" message on his video screen. Regardless, my youngest son relentlessly pressed the restart button that eventually led him to complete the game with an overwhelming victory.

In perspective, challenges in human interaction is inescapable due to our human frailty. Things beyond our control are expected because the world we live in is not perfect either.

When things turned sour, building walls around us or throwing in the towel tend to be the easy way out in coping with life's relationships. We must keep on pressing the restart button and persistently stay in the game of life.

Forgiveness is God's restart button. When we forgive, it is not for the sake of the other party; forgiveness is for our benefit. Others may cause us to stumble, falter, and trip over; but we can repeatedly forgive.

Press God's restart button and keep on forgiving. It is the way for our faith to breakthrough.

The Means to Get Us Going

Pending to the full expression of our freedom in Christ is our forgiveness of others. When we do, the path of possibilities towards the future fling wide open. You see, God forged our future because His grace of forgiveness already shapes our past.

Indifference is the reason why transformation is not the concern of significance to the person with a hardened heart. Nonetheless, we know that without the renewal of our soul, we cannot move on in life.

To stay in course towards on fully seeing the plans and purposes of God manifest in our lives; our forgiveness of people who have caused us pain is the cross where we put our flesh where it rightfully belongs; of course, under the subjection of our born-again spirit.

If we believe in the grace of God, then the expected result of that belief is, we too will be gracious to our offenders. Grace is beyond a doctrine; it is a practical virtue. You cannot help but be gracious when you are full of the Spirit of Grace.[127]

Unforgiveness is the exact opposite of who God is. Harboring grudges is a spiritual corrosion that litters our hearts with an offense. Such carnal decay can get in the way of God's divine flow. To tap the supernatural, our underlying principle of operation must be something that represents who God is. God is love, and through His love, we can forgive.

Forgiveness is a Form of Giving of Self

Sandwiched in the word forgiveness is the word give. Forgiveness remains as a fuzzy religious ideal unless it is given away.

Forgiveness is outstretching the grace and mercy of God to the undeserving. It involves a follow through of handing commitment of forbearance.

When God forgave the unlovable world of its sin, He gave up the very life of His Son; the God's only begotten became the substitute for His judgment of our sin.

In the same manner, we abandon our sense of entitlement, and we amplify our consideration that we are already dead unto sin but alive unto God whenever we lay down our pride to forgive. Nothing quickly reenacts Christ's victory over strife than forgiveness.

Transformation precedes our society when those who claimed to understand the Way, walks the grace of extra mile, and turned the other cheek of forbearance instead of the hurt cheek of our ego. God's love breaks down every barrier.

As the expression of grace's forgiveness emit a sweet-smelling aroma of worship, the residue of pride that sits in our emotion and in our reasoning is burned. Grace and self-entitlement can never be on the same crowd.

Let us wake up to the fact that the Church – the Body of Christ is the sole demonstrator of God's grace on this planet. Our Father in heaven is merciful and gracious; as His children, grace and mercy are our inheritance to demonstrate to our sphere of influence. The one standing in the way of God to bless the world is the residue of selfishness and pride illegally squatting in our soul.

God and His blessing cannot go side by side with any form of pride. What makes God to nauseate allegorically speaking is a lukewarm heart causes by pride.

Unforgiveness is not justifiable when God by His grace, pardoned us from our grave sin. Unforgiveness is a spiritual prison that incessantly restricts us until the Lord opens His mercy and grace to our understanding.

Check the Roots

For years, a serious issue of anger lurks under my nose. When I left the East Coast back in 2001, my temper gets quickly flares up even with slightest of aggravation. This chronic spiritual problem took the best of me in the winter of 2011 when I confronted my eldest son. To make the story short, I ended up provoking my son to severe anger.

When all the smoke settled down so to speak, I was miserable, and I was desperately telling God that I am tired of getting angry constantly. Suddenly, deep inside me, I heard a spontaneous word; "check the roots!" As these spoken words arrested all my awareness to a complete halt, a familiar countenance flashed before my face. In my dismay, I immediately asked God; "Did you mean to tell me that I have to fly to East Coast and deal with this guy again?"

Deep inside, the witness of God's peace assured my heart that it is a green light and it is a good time to go. As soon as I arrived in New York weeks later, I get in touched with my former Pastor and tried to arrange a meeting with him.

Back in October of 1996, I came here in the U.S. with only $200 in my pocket. I knew that coming to America is God's divine agenda for spiritual training and discipline as the Lord told me in a dream. US Immigration only stamped my passport with six months of legal stay.

Before my visa expires, I prayed to God to have His way in letting me stay in America legally, or I will go back to the Philippines. Not long after I made known such specific request to our Father God, a friend of mine brought me to a church in New Jersey.

Chapter 9: The Catalyst for Breakthrough

This congregation just got out of a major split. Thus, their worship ministry was in shamble. Their church's ministerial situation became an opportunity for my friend to recommend me to the church's board.

Accordingly, they unanimously voted me in and agreed to process my immigration documents. From December of 1995 until the early part of 1999, I stayed and served the said church. I got my green card six months after we applied for it. The result was faster than expected.

While working in the church in the capacity of an Associate Pastor, one day the Pastor told me that the church has no plans in sponsoring my family to come over to the US. He further told to me; it is all up to me to bring them over; although they can sponsor my family, the Pastor opted not to.

I struggled to keep myself afloat from the financial stipend that I was receiving from the church. They had me stay temporarily from church's member house unto another. Since the pastor relegated the responsibility of bringing over my family into the US on my concern, I had no other choice but to leave the church after serving it from 1995 to 1999.

Staying in New Jersey was not feasible to have another job on the side and stay with the church at the same time. To satisfy the requirement of the US Immigration in sponsoring my family, New York is the only viable place to get it done because of 24-hour access to public transportation, not to mention the availability and the proximity to jobs.

I could choose to stay in the church that petitioned me, but that will compromise the principle of providing for my household as a husband and a father. I have no other choice but to leave the said church even though that contradicts the Pastor's expectation.

While living in New York, I continued to help my friend's Assembly of God church in Brooklyn and Staten Island to at least maintain my written and signed agreement with the US Immigration.

Now, fast-forward to winter of 2011, days before I flew to New York, a snowstorm struck and knocked down some of the power lines in the North Jersey area. I called the said Pastor, and he told me that he cannot accommodate me because of the absence of electricity in their house; and at that time, they were staying at his daughter's place.

Unable to come over to where he is, I have no choice but to deal everything over the phone. I apologized for leaving the church short of three years after I received my green card. As soon as I uttered those words, his intense anger resonated all over my ears.

My first inclination was to give him a piece of my mind and verbally get even with him and shove in his face all the things that I am not at privilege to say in this book, but the Lord gently nudged me to be quiet despite all his verbal poundings. I told him that the Lord wants me to go back in the ministry and I gently asked him to pray a prayer of release for me. To my surprise, he did and prayed over me a beautiful prayer.

Right after he concluded his prayer; he went back where his anger left off, and for good measure, he lashed me out more with verbal whippings. He then told me, "You have to come tomorrow at the church service and stand behind the pulpit and ask forgiveness to the congregation!"

I told the Lord; "I have come this far from Alaska to East Coast, I can go all the way if you want me to do this Pastor's bidding, but if it is not your will, make a way that these things will not happen." On the inside, I knew that the said Pastor would like to have me as his trophy to exact his self-entitlement.

Chapter 9: The Catalyst for Breakthrough

When I hung up the phone, a pastor friend of mine who sits right beside me stated: "the New York Marathon will close the Verrazano Bridge from 6 am to 4 pm Sunday morning tomorrow, there is no way in and no way out." I said, "Okay Lord, that's one witness, I need at least one more witness to establish that it is not your will for me to go."

For a second witness, I specifically asked God that somebody would invite me to preach in their church service. If things did not turn out otherwise, I would drive my way to the said church regardless of how long it will take me to get there. Even though I have no familiarity of the route, I resolute to use the back road just to show up in the said church.

As I kept an eye like a hawk on my mobile phone to ring up, nobody called me from Saturday night until passed 1 of Sunday morning; then I finally gave up waiting. As I retired to bed and determined to drive to New Jersey early in the morning, guess what? My cell phone rang at exactly two o'clock in the morning. It was another Pastor acquaintance of mine, and he requested me to preach in their Sunday Church Service. Who in the world will call you at two o'clock in the morning unless it is God's doing?

I thanked God for making His will so clear. I accepted the preaching invitation, and right away I sent a text message to the New Jersey pastor and told him that it is not possible for me to get pass through Verrazano Bridge because of New York Marathon.

For sure, the Lord's hand was orchestrating everything about my soul's brokenness pending to its breakthrough, as I tried to give account to series of events that took place. All the while, the Lord is waiting for me to demonstrate my sense of willingness to presses in regardless.

That Sunday I preached the sermon the Lord personally gave me on; "Lessons on John 3:16" which I am now in the process of working as a book project. I felt rusty as I was preaching at my friend's church that Sunday, for I have not done such because of years of absence in the ministry. However, by the grace of God, the message preached was so personally liberating; "It is good to be back in the land of the living." Hallelujah to God Almighty!

Deliverance comes in many forms; mine came through by obeying the Spirit of God. The following Monday I flew back to Anchorage, Alaska and I felt tons of anger lifted off me. It was not just a relief, but it is a sense of spiritual freedom. Not many days after, I received a download from God, which serves as a green light in writing this book. We also came across a financial breakthrough at that month, where we received three separate checks in the mail in the total amount of $23,000.

In 2011, despite of President Barack Obama's stimulus money to jumpstart construction business; my boss had to laid me off because those days were economically tough for any construction firm all over America. I have been looking for a job for months and months since the engineering firm that I worked with for three years laid me off, but I was unsuccessful in landing even a job interview.

After I came back from New York, I received a revelation on Matthew 6 particularly on verse 33. In my excitement, I told my wife that I am not going to look for a job anymore, but instead jobs will come looking for me. Days after this revelatory encounter from God, my family and I attended a friend's church. A gentleman from the said church greeted and personally asked me if I am presently working; I candidly said: "no I am not." He asked for my cell phone number and to make the story short; I got an IT contractual job that I have no experience at all. The said job paid a handsomely amount of money, almost triple the amount of what I was making on my last gig at the engineering firm. Hallelujah!

I came to the realization that if Jesus' Kingship and His righteousness becomes the first place in our hearts, then all of His blessings will start seeking us." Making King Jesus our priority affects our lives in the Kingdom, this translates into the King seeing us well represented and well provided. Again, I say; "blessings will come as supplementary when we make His Lordship and His righteousness our priority."

Our breakthrough hinges on our forgiveness of others. When we forgive, we discharge ourselves from every hold of the enemy and that token of commitment opens the gate valve of God's blessings to flow down on us.

Check the roots. When the roots are healthy, you will bear fruits in plenty. Hallelujah! Our forgiveness is a catalyst for our breakthrough.

CHAPTER TEN
Keep on Breaking It Through
The other side is awaiting our breakthrough

Launching Out into the Deep

> *...He said to Simon, "Launch out into the deep..."*
>
> Luke 5:4 NKJV

Following their all-nighter unsuccessful fishing expedition, Jesus entreated Simon to borrow his boat and asked to be pushed a little farther from the shore to create a buffer zone between Him and the unruly crowd.

Jesus started teaching the people, and when He is done sharing His heart, the Lord told Simon to go back to the sea and to let down his net for a catch.

Jesus' directives contradict the known fishing paradigm of the time. Net- casting in dark hours with the use of a fire on illuminating the waters around the boat is fisherman's method of madness in luring and bringing the school of fish; this system has been their known trade's best practice passed down to them by their forefathers.

I mean for crying out loud, Simon is a seasoned fisherman, and Jesus is just a carpenter! Right? Exactly! What does He know about fishing? In an unlikely hour, Jesus ridiculously told Simon to go back into the deep for a catch.

There must be something on Jesus' teaching that primed Simon's heart to relinquish all-natural reasoning for a venture of faith believing. He said, "...we toiled all night, nonetheless at your Word; we will let down our net again."

The words 'launch out' in Luke 5:4 is a compound Greek word "epanago." 'Epi' means 'across or through' and 'anago' signifies "to launch."[128] So, the full implication of the word is "to propel across or to pierce through." The transliteration depicts a picture of a spear being thrust through from one side onto the other side.

When Jesus spoke; "...launch out into the deep;" Jesus was telling Simon to launch his faith like a spear going through the natural human disposition and off to the other side where God's supernatural provision of great harvests was all along waiting for his breakthrough. The manifestation of our breakthrough is a result of our agreement with God.

Here is one thing that we need to value and understand; God's provision is not the following effect of our belief. The Lord has been waiting for us to believe on the level of who we already are in Christ. Our faith does not determine who God is, for He already determined our identity in Christ back in the eternity past.

The Lord's provision precedes human need way before there was time. Our action does not get to decide what God is about to move. His abundant supply is already a settled fact on the other side; they are all waiting for our breakthrough.

Simon propelled his faith beyond the human reasoning of "successful fishing can't be carried out during the daytime hour." Faith dawned on Simon's heart, and he perceived the reality of seeing himself harvesting a significant catch after hearing the spoken Words of Jesus; "...launch out into the deep."

The ability to see himself in a completed condition by way of revelation, is what the abovementioned scriptures is highlighting on us. Indeed, into the depths of Jesus' Words, Simon's faith was launched for a momentous harvest.

Respectively, the external yield of Simon's inward conviction was way beyond his natural capacity to accommodate, he needed to summon others to help in reaping the enormous harvest.

When we hold nothing back and dive into the depths of Jesus' revelation, then our reception of His blessings will be beyond what we can contain. Ultimately, our heavenly favored rewards also benefit those who are around us.

When our crosshair marked the target, and we accordingly pulled the trigger, then what breaks through the flight path is the launched projectile; ultimately it hits the objective.

In Christ, what launches us off to our divine destiny is the engagement of faith. The trajectory of our faith is rather intentional and not accidental. When the vision of faith is perceived, the realization of God's purpose is what our spirit lays hold to manifest.

A Holy Spirit's given insight opens the eyes of our understanding to see beyond the restriction of the natural realm. Revelation is indeed glimpsing into our possibilities in Christ.

Nothing propels our identity to our destiny than the revealed knowledge of the heart of God. Our personal encounter with the One who called us settles our focus to be passionate about His purpose. Human intelligence alone is incapable of incarnating such calling.

Since God invested into our spirit everything that pertains to life and godliness through the merit of the shed blood of Christ, then what is remain for the world to witness is the tangible manifestation of our soul's spiritual breakthrough. Greater things await us on the other side; it is more glorious than where we currently at in the natural.

His substance authenticates us when we recognize the Father as our source. His grace empowers us to launch ourselves into the depths of His purpose. His goodness leads us to the absolute path of repentance, and it propels our faith to walk with Him.

Complication: The Great Divide

Straightforward things are easy to comprehend; on the other hand, complexity is full of drama. Simplicity focuses on essentials.

Today Jesus is still saying to us; "…only believe." What the Lord is telling us will not get more straightforward than that! Another plainly way of looking such phrase is "…believe only." Funny huh?

When the Lord Jesus came into this world, he is not trying to impress us. He is already God when we were not yet around, and He remains as such after we are all long earthly gone. The Lord does not need our help on super spiritualizing His Words, all we need is to take Him at His Word.

Getting into the promise land was never intended to be 40 years of marathon run around the same wilderness' mountain. Jehovah's divine intention is to get the Jewish nation to Canaan in no time. Instead of taking God at His Word, Israel tried to figure how they can help God out.

Forthright direction can only be executed with simple submission. However, unpleasant delays are looming on the horizon as we seek to insert our ways to what specifically God wanted our faith to take on.

Make no mistake about this! When by revelation we got a hold of our destiny in Christ, the pursuit of His purpose is no longer a complication, but it is now a matter of pressing in for your spiritual breakthrough. Indeed, the Holy Spirit revealed knowledge is a force multiplier.

We are no longer in the stance of crowding ourselves to Jesus in trying to get His attention. His truth sets us free, and we now see ourselves connected with His everlasting virtue.

As His revelation opens our heart up, the flow of His eternity to our world of temporary makes the impossible possible and spins human assumed burdens as light and easy. His everlasting goodness rolls our life around from usual unto the phenomenal.

As our demarcated life is ticking down its time, we cannot stand still and suspends ourselves on the sideline. We are mandated to press on to our true calling. Our faith must be carried on in occupying this world with the good news of His Kingdom. We are His forerunners, and we prepare the way for the King to come back for His own.

Yes, there is still battle for us to gain grounds within the arena of our soul, but it is a fight of keeping what Jesus initiated, succeeded, and completed on His great redemption. It is a good fight of faith. It is the race where our faith presses on for the highest calling; in which we are possessing the perfection for which the Lord Jesus Christ first possessed us, our soul transfiguring like Him in this world.[129]

Running the Race of Faith

> Not that I have already attained, or am already perfected; but I press on, that I may lay hold of that for which Christ Jesus has also laid hold of me. Brethren, I do not count myself to have apprehended; but one thing I do, forgetting those things which are behind and reaching forward to those things which are ahead, I press toward the goal for the prize of the upward call of God in Christ Jesus.
>
> *Philippians 3:12-14 NKJV*

By deliberately mentioning the word "press" twice on these passages of scriptures, Apostle Paul highlighted his line of thoughts regarding his pursuit of God's purpose. The said word is a present active infinitive Greek verb "diokos" means to run swiftly,[130] This all applies to us.

Therefore, "diokos" depicts an image of a sprinter who rapidly dashes towards the finish line. Sprint race comprise of three stages. Understanding these steps gives us the snapshot of a spiritual trajectory towards the purposes of God. These phases are propelling, pressing on, and breaking out.

Propelling

In the sprint race, propelling your body to run from a vertically 90° straight from the ground position pulls your weight downward by gravity. It is gruesome to initially dash from this stance; this will quickly wear your energy out. As the sprinter prepare to launch; his hands are on the ground, and his feet are set to catapult onward from starting blocks.

The science for this running position is to slingshot an athlete from a strong start. The sprinter takeoff to the fire of the gun, like a spear piercing through the elements, he catapults his body forwardly leaning 60° to the ground. Propelling in such way harnesses gravity, body mass, muscle memory, the elements, and the running distance to work for sprinter's advantage. Such running posture is intentional by design.

In perspective, we deliberately harness oppositions for our advantage when by revelation we embark on our inner conviction in Christ. Since the blood of Christ already rigged the game of life on our favor, external aggravation means nothing to us anymore; for we are catapulting towards our destiny based on our established destiny in Christ.

Problems served as an assembly line where we can piece together components of God's solution that He already consummated and fulfilled. During challenges, things are not disintegrating, but they are shaping up towards the actuality of our purpose when we choose to respond in faith.

We indeed still fight the good fight of faith, but it is a good fight because we engage in a battle from the stance of Jesus' victory. We propel in life from the benefits of why Jesus shed His blood on the cross.

Pressing In

When the sprinter is on the run, he presses on against pressure with pressure. His arms, shoulders, legs and breathing patterns are all in one synchronized rhythm. His forward front leg along with his coordinated forward front arm presses in, while his backward rear leg along with his synchronized back rear arm pushes out. The sprinter pushes back the ground behind as he presses on forward to reach more frontal grounds.

In effect, Apostle Paul said; "…forgetting those things which are behind and reaching to those things which are before." Beloved, the new things that we forwardly propel ourselves unto is what pushes back the old things that we leave behind.

Though old things have been passed away from the viewpoint of our new creation spirit in Christ, yet there are residues of our past's life that are still lingering in our mind, emotions, and will. Carnal dispositions in our soul can make us feel all lies of the enemy as believable if we are not vigilant in the spirit.

Granted that our recreated spirits are already complete in Christ but the reason why our soul was left undone after we got born again, is for us to have an opportunity to engage who we are in Christ in this world.

The ever-increasing greatness of God who indwells us is the force the world will come to reckon with, when from the inside out we enforce our faith over our sight. Our soul's transformation is the prime reason why we are here in this world. The process of renewing our mind is what putting on the new man in Christ over the carnal mind is all about.

Breaking Out

From the early stage of the race, a wise sprinter will maintain a regular rate of pressing in and pressing out until the perfect timing queues him to break everything out he has on the inside and ultimately cross the finish line in victory.

Because of God's purpose, the manifestation of faith is for a timely season. Breakthrough is a process of transitioning who we are in the realm of the spirit onto the natural. God's revealed knowledge propel our conviction into a relentless passion for our soul's spiritual breakthrough.

Transitioning from Interruptions

Disruption is a crucible where we can experience the God who worked inside of us will be the same Father who flow through us. God's monument (testimony) of greatness on our lives are practically built by stones the world thrown against us.

By His divine favor, we can transition our interruptions into manifesting God's provision. Thus, His grace could only mean this, His willingness and ability to bring our soul to His fullness.

We go past further than our comfort zone and launches our faith to our designation of influence when we let the Holy Spirit's revelation pitches us into the greater understanding why Jesus died on the cross.

Life eternal commenced at the new birth; however, engaging our faith to His purpose is what consummates His manifested glory to dawn on our soul. We can only find the divine expression of our identity through God's calling and Christ's allocated grace.

From His presence, God's wisdom is available to flow through us when we choose to position our soul to receive. The Holy Spirit's outflowed wisdom is God's equalizer to any interruptions.

What divinely enlightened us becomes our assignment's solution. Yes, amid a raging storm, the presence of Jesus is in the same boat with us. To gets us to our manifested destiny that awaits us on the other side, let us stand our ground and speak His peace – His divine order – in front of raging interruptions.

God's calling provides accommodation for growth and equipment for service. When we plug in relationally with the Holy Spirit, all things become beautiful because we are flowing in His timing. In our pursuit of our upward calling in Christ, we must disregard the preceding to take advantage of the upcoming. Our life in Christ is a series of pressing on.

Each progressive manifestation of glory, each momentum of faith, and each remarkable revelation of grace leads us to a greater measure. Only Christ's revelation can further our soul beyond where we were before. Each unfolding stages of divine favor are exhilarating and exciting.

Living in an Imperfect World with our Perfect God

Since God is with us, stands for us, and lives within us; oppositions, therefore, can be exploited for our advantage. When the grace of God revealed an awareness of the life that God gave us through the precious blood of Christ. Life surely gives rise to an out of this world expression.

No longer we breathe life from the strain of trying to keep up a self-made spirituality. Rather, we are resonating life of what God has given us in Christ. Such life celebrates joy in every imaginable expression. Yes, even defecating is an all-time enjoyable past time because what is filling our hearts is the appreciation of God for every life's detail.

What protects a submarine from potential implosion due to the sea depth's weighty compression is its internal pressure system that counters the external constraining force. Moreover, finding the treasure within our hearts is worth more than losing our minds due to our external challenges.

The One who indwells us is greater than all external worldly opposition. Fear has torment, but freedom is radiated from the heart of whose trust is in God's love.

Life is a journey; it is a series of faith transition. Our next breakthrough is well underway; we just keep on propelling, pressing in, and breaking out because our soul's ultimate completion awaits us at the other side.

The target always gets hit because of the marksman connection to his line of sight. We always find our divine envisioned expression when from the inside, we see ourselves who we are in Christ.

Becoming Dissatisfiedly Satisfied

How can we press on with our destiny if just passing small victories is what fixates us? Pathetic life is not wholesome neither worthwhile. The good things that God began in our lives culminate when our soul aligns with our true being in Christ.

Again, there is more to our soul ahead of us than the less of what we currently are. Let us seek for more of God until the less of who we are in our soul realm is consummated with His fullness.

In response to Jesus' summon and pending to Bartimaeus' receipt of breakthrough, he yanked off and threw his begging coat aside. He knew by revelation that in receiving his miracle of sight, an old cloak is no longer needed.

As he gave precedence and recognition to Jesus Kingly position; "…Jesus, son of David, have mercy on me," a divine revelation dawned in his heart. He declared; "I am through with this life of darkness and restriction. I am not begging anymore. With Christ miracle, I am propelling myself to my new identity."[131] If Bartimaeus pressed on to make it his own, so should we!

In effect, he was saying; "this is my time, nobody can take this one away from me; regardless how are other people are trying to count me out based on their significance, I am moving on to make it as my own.

Today is my moment, this is my new season, and this is my God's time. Step away religious pushovers: this is my time to breakthrough."

Seizing Our Moments with God

> …For the Lord does not see as man sees; for man looks at the outward appearance, but the Lord looks at the heart.
>
> 1 Samuel 16:7 NKJV

The nation of Israel framed their expectation of the coming Christ based on the prophecy that the Messiah will sprout from the roots of Jesse (King David's father). They expected Him to come by way of the entrance of a royal stallion. However, Jesus became their biggest party crasher when He showed up riding on a donkey in the form of a servant.

What a big disappointment it was! Given that, Jesus is the Lion of the tribe of Judah and yet He came into this world as a sacrificial lamb by the will of His Father.

Jesus ultimately compounded the liberal's worldly wisdom and the conservative's religious strength through the weak and the foolish proclamation of God's Kingdom.

The spiritual lesson of the story is regardless of our relentless religiosity, we cannot make God slip His BIG feet into our tiny shoes. Our carnal sophistication often blunders our sensing of God's visitation.

It will cost us the opportunity of seizing our moments with God when we are so adamant in matching our expectation with our external assumption.

When it comes to expecting a spiritual breakthrough, are we aware of it by the eye of faith or by the attitude of reason? We spirally suck in into a whirlpool of disillusion and confusion every time we try negotiating spiritual things by way of sight and reason. Nonetheless, when we live through the faith of the Son, we flow where we are divinely connected. God's blessings are not the issue anymore because Christ's resurrection power is abundantly available within us.

His greatness inside of us supplied us the ability to capture our earthly Christ revealed possibilities. However, when the Holy Spirit enlightened our souls with the understanding of God's ways and His thoughts, our God given moments then becomes apparent. If you can perceive that you already have it, then you can manifest it.

Chapter 10: Keep on Breaking it Through

No can do, God is even greater beyond concepts that we can dare imagine or think. Now to Him who is able to do exceedingly abundantly above all that we ask or think, according to the power that works in us.

Ephesians 3:20 The Message Bible

The same power that raised Jesus from the dead is inherently available within those who are in Christ. Nevertheless, tapping unto such degree of God's purpose where the overwhelming power of the Spirit manifests, such state of life involves the restoration of our soul. Salvation is purely by grace but streaming through the rivers of the Holy Spirit's anointing comes with the price of mind renewal. Moreover, God the Father is willing to share His ability to places and condition beyond where a carnal mind can dare step into.

Religion is so accustomed to doing things the hard way. Nevertheless, the lightness reception of God's grace always opposes man's religious comprehension. All that Jesus lived, died, and resurrected for is the established truth of the New Covenant. The Gospel is God's rest and liberation for our soul. The wholeness of Christ resurrection life within our spirit is ready to swallow the remaining corrupt residues in our soul.

God desires to restore everything that Adam lost in the garden; in that regard, that includes the restoration of man's original condition of his soul – the soul that fused with God's Spirit. The entire creation is intensely waiting for the global flow of the Spirit through our new creation spirit aligned soul. The essential part of spiritual breakthrough is the breaking of the carnal mind's comfort zone.

What hinders us from realizing our purpose in Christ is our emotional attachment to what we sentimentalized as real but never even once an actual deal. The whole template of God's divine purpose is wrapped up in the life, death, and resurrection of Jesus; failing to seize this divine purpose is worse than death. There is no alternative for the Jesus life.

Esau completely lost his claim to his destiny when he chose bread and lentils over his birthright. The link that connects the incompleteness of our soul to the entirety of life eternal inside our spirits is the revelation of who Christ is on the inside of us.

Unless we allow the Holy Spirit's illumination in dismantling the worldly and demonic interferences that garrison in our soul, we will continue to operate as the world does. Carnal structure decomposes our soul's persona. Breaking through the mind of carnality is our spiritual mandate from God.

> *Whereby are given unto us exceeding great and precious promises: that by these ye might be partakers of the divine nature, having escaped the corruption that is in the world through lust.*
>
> *2 Peter 1:4 KJV*

Religion will try to achieve spirituality by natural means. Pursuing life's divine intention through religious doctrine and tradition is not only stiff, but it is also unattainable. We cannot spiritually posture ourselves by natural means because the stance of the recreated spirit always opposed the appetites of the flesh.

The problem points us to the solution. The problem can never be the solution. You cannot replace the eternal with something temporal. In the natural, Our DNA is what defines our physical heritage. Likewise, our spiritual DNA is our identity, calling, conviction, and destiny in Christ. Jesus is the answer to our problem. He is the solution that completes our insufficiency.

We cannot outclass who Jesus is. He is the perfect theology of all time. Deep inside the heart of every child of God, there is recognition of the sense of significance of who he is in Christ.

It is an awareness of something greater than what you presently are in your soul. In the inner recesses of your being, there is a yearning that cries out with deafening urgency, an inward perception that is laying hold on something unknown to the finite mind, but undeniably authentic conviction from within.

When we got saved, the attribute of God's divine nature was spiritually built-in within us. The Spirit of God has imparted an essence of destiny and purpose inside us.

There is nothing else satisfies our sense of destiny and calling than the visitation of God's glory. Only the presence of God and the revelation of the Word of God can fill our soul. Have you ever wondered why the Bible refer God as the Lover of our soul?[132]

The progression of our soul's spiritual breakthrough is a part of God's eternal plan on earth. We start manifesting our God-given potential when by faith we engage the plan of God for humanity and the world.

The Church is an integral part of the eternal purposes of God. Without the Body of Christ growing into the eternal purposes of God, the plan of God is held back and delayed.

You Manifest What You Behold

> *Nevertheless when one turns to the Lord, the veil is taken away. Now the Lord is the Spirit; and where the Spirit of the Lord is, there is liberty. But we all, with unveiled face, beholding as in the mirror the glory of the Lord, are being transformed into the same image from glory to glory, just as by the Spirit of the Lord.*
>
> *2 Corinthians 3:16-18 NKJV*

Sin veils the spiritual eyes of those who are outside of God's Kingdom. Spiritual blindness incapacitates the world from seeing the glory of Jesus. Nonetheless, the scales of ignorance fall off their spiritual eyes when they turned to the Lord, and this results to gazing the glory of Christ so freely.

When we honor and recognize the preeminence of the Holy Spirit's presence, it liberates us to see the life transforming glory of God. When by His Spirit we break through the casing of our human limitation, God's divine intention burst into our lives with extraordinary passion.

Truth forms in our soul when we start believing the right thing. Our divine destiny shapes our humanity, as we continually gaze on Christ's glory.

People misfire because they failed to engage their belief unto their intended goal. Apostle Paul said, "thus I fight: not as one who beats the air."

Inside the ring, a boxer takes on his contender. Such time is not the right place to do shadow boxing. We secure the manifestation of our victory when we keep on focusing on faith's sole direction.

Our calling is our God's prophetic vision. In the natural, when you summon somebody, you must use your voice in calling that individual out. In the same token, there is no calling without a spoken word. God's personal spoken word to you is your God's prophetic vision – your God-given spiritual focus. Jesus is our Alpha and Omega; He is the beginning and the end; He sandwiched us and everything in between.

Christ sustains our spiritual focus from the initiation to consummation. Looking through His eyes enables us to envision and manifest our divine identity.

Learning from Simon Peter

For as long as Simon Peter gazes on Jesus and clings on His revelatory word "come," he miraculously walked on water. Nonetheless, tapping on the supernatural is not an exemption to temptation; even more you become a prime target of the wiles of the enemy.

Fear camouflagely crept in as a wind that blows and water rolling its biggest waves, as soon as Simon entertained it he started sinking for he switched from the realm of God unto the realm that can be influence by the adversary.

I can imagine that the eleven disciples back in the boat were sarcastically giggling when Simon Peter blew a supernatural activity once again; as if they were a sort of "Oh, oh! Simon rides again."

Among the twelve, Simon Peter was the only one who is more open to the supernatural. Nobody got it first but him because he was more curious than the whole gang was.

Until the day of the Pentecost, Peter did not have a well-defined purpose why following Jesus is important and relevant. Simon Peter's relationship with Jesus at that time was more of acquaintance; he was just hanging out with the coolest guy in Israel.

Simon Peter's approach to temptation is to fight it through with his own strength rather than engaging it based on what Jesus told him. Thus, his self-confidence-based focus often puts him into trouble.

His self-generated approach procured a spiritual roller coaster ride. At one time, he was up confessing Jesus as the Messiah and then being rebuke as Satan the next time. He was courageous to cut someone's ear off and then became coward to a little girl's inquiry. This only tells us; that earthly strength and wits burns out when it does, it cannot even withstand an insignificant life's challenges.

Faith is a commitment to abandon a boatload of unbelief and to boldly launch into the spiritual depths of the Lord Jesus Christ. Focus is a dynamic component of faith. Faith apprehends the unseen; it is our homing radar during the storms of life.

Going down to moral ditches is more likely when faith is deprived of its inspiration; without warning disruptions will try in getting us when we lay down our guard.

The noise of interruptions is silent by the faith aimed on what is laying hold unto. What your soul is ultimately capable of becoming in the Kingdom of God commenced in the heart and the mind of God long before He created all things and Jesus ratified it as legally yours by shedding His blood. The ultimate you are what Christ Jesus rendered entirely at the cross and His resurrection.

Chapter 10: Keep on Breaking it Through

> *He has made everything beautiful in its time. He also has PLANTED ETERNITY IN MEN'S HEART and minds [a divinely implanted sense of a purpose working through the ages which nothing under the sun but God alone can satisfy]...*
>
> *Ecclesiastes 3:11 Amplified Bible*

There is no such thing as out of focus. Life in all categories is a matter of interest. One way or another, we fix our heart on something beneficial or something destructive. We should be careful on where our minds dwells on.

We may lean towards sudden nonsensical carnal urges when we relax our guard. We manifest what we behold. We should all stick with just one focus of gazing – which is the glory of the Lord. Many times, we are beholding on the wrong kinds of stuff, and ended up representing unwanted dispositions.

Yes, we happen to carry out the things where our mind focuses. Wrong focus means the wrong direction, and the wrong direction means the wrong destination. Focusing only on the truth is an efficient way of living our life.

Executing the essentials saves us time to fight against pointless things. Mainly, our struggles stem from focusing on the wrong things. If we are going forward, we are not going backward. Exactly!

Are we still focusing on fighting the fight that Jesus won for us already? Are we fixing our eyes on the glory of Jesus' championship ring? Fighting the non-essential is the same as a basketball player who keeps shooting the ball on the hoop of the opposing team, he keeps on scoring points, but he is piling it up against his own team.

It is an exercise in futility to fight the battle that already been won; such useless religious performance brushes away the awareness of the joy of our divine relationship with our Savior.

Focusing on our destiny eliminates the time we spend fighting the unnecessary. The life of God's Kingdom should be a rerun of Christ's exploits and victory. Guys we live on what Christ already won for us; we do not settle for losing. Winning makes life worthwhile!

Breaking Forth into Joy

> *But I want you to know, brethren, that the things which happened to me have actually turned out for the furtherance of the Gospel, so that it has become evident to the whole palace guard, and to all the rest, that my chains are in Christ; and most of the brethren in the Lord, having become confident by my chains, are much more bold to speak the word without fear. Some indeed preach Christ even from envy and strife, and some also from goodwill: The former preach Christ from selfish ambition, not sincerely, supposing to add affliction to my chains; but the latter out of love, knowing that I am appointed for the defense of the Gospel. What then? Only that in every way, whether in pretense or in truth, Christ is preached; and in this I rejoice, yes, and will rejoice.*
>
> *Philippians 1:13-18 KJV*

When we understand that our God the Father cannot be confined by earthly restrictions, chaotic urgencies become occasions for our breakthrough.

By getting the mind of Christ concerning his situation, Paul broke the Gospel through into the most inaccessible place in his time – the Roman palace. His opposition became an opportunity for breaking forth into the joy of many. We can always expect God's intervention amid temptations.

When Paul glimpsed into the mind of Christ regarding his incarceration, his perspective shifted from a condition of setback unto the occasion of God's unique creative solution. The prison became his staging point to accomplish the will of God.

He bragged on what the world may look as an occasion of defeat as his opportunity to explore God's immeasurable wisdom. Instead of being constantly nagged by his imprisonment, he confidently declared, "…my chains are in Christ…"

Paul was probably saying; "my spirit is free though this jail contains me physically; but none of these things moves me." The revelation of the power of Christ's resurrection compelled Paul to press on and invade the whole palace with the Gospel of Christ.

Our restriction is an occasion for God to outline His marvelous grace in our lives. Most of the writing that Paul did, he wrote them within the grounds of his prison's restriction.

God has a greater picture in mind; with Paul having his freedom to preach the gospel it can only reach his known world at the time. Nonetheless, having his time devoted in communing with God inside the prison, he received a revelation that was written that reach the modern world which is way beyond his time.

In Case You Fell in Between the Cracks

Often, our stiff-necked mentality is being knocked out by life's reality. Moreover, God by His sovereignty will time and again use the things that we pride ourselves off to be our painful wake-up call.

Truth often slaps our face with sensibility. Nobody realizes their flaw until after their undealt soul's persona gives them a blackeye.

All across-the-board, human interaction is complex. Life does not have just two sides; there are more sides to life than meets the eye. Pride makes someone feel that he is invincible and considers the world revolves around him and thus becoming insensitive to people that surrounds him.

Pride keeps us from discerning the many peripheries of life, ignorance of such leads to relational challenges. Pride ticks like a time bomb, in due course; its inevitability explodes right before the proud man's face. However, this is where the Blood of the Lamb comes into play in the landscape of human frailty.

God knows our frame and the forgiveness which He wrought in Christ is more than sufficient to cover our tracks, shelter our current failures, and shields us from things that we can stumble in the future. Jesus is already our beginning and our completion. When we somehow messed up and fall, we are still a part of what He began and His agenda of what He completed on the cross. Get up, dust yourself off, and let your soul keep on pressing.

After his divorce, a friend of mine told me that it would take him a while to get back to what he used to be doing in the ministry. For him, recapturing his former moments of glory is his queue for his biggest return. I told him; "You don't have to! Jesus took all your shame and replaced it with His glory."

Everything that Jesus accomplished for us is all matter of faith stance, and we rest on what Jesus has done. In the game of life, what is important is not the way we stumble and fall, but the way the game is wrapped up.

Just like Samson, God is faithful to enable us to cross the finish line with a significant bang! Our fall can also be our opportunity for breakthrough.

From Breakthrough to Breakthrough

The Kingdom of God has three stages of revelation: the entrance, the inheritance, and the culmination. Experiencing the inheritance of the Kingdom is what fills the gap between the entry and culmination of the Kingdom.

The entrance of the Kingdom is what happened to our spirits when we got born again. Experiencing Kingdom's inheritance is where our soul transformation occurs; lastly, the culmination of the Kingdom on the earth will transpire at the second coming of our King.

Spiritual breakthrough is synonymous to the transfiguration of our soul; we become in our soul who we already are in our spirits. Our soul transfigures unto the likeness of Jesus from glory to glory. Our mind, emotion, and will increases from strength to strength.

Life in God's Kingdom is a journey; it is a series of faith transition. We are getting established on the understanding of God's righteousness from faith to faith, from grace upon grace, and from glory to glory. Series of breakthroughs happens in between faith's inception and culmination.

Our soul grows from breakthrough to breakthrough. Our soul's spiritual growth is a series of leaving and emerging. Each stage is a precursor to the next. Every level constituted a new further understanding of the same truth.

Just like climbing a ladder, it expands our horizon each time we go up one step higher. To give way to the new, relinquishing our comfort zone is imperative.

Faith is what links eternity to our temporal existence. Crucial to our soul's spiritual growth is the continuity of divine faith life. As Apostle Paul said, "...in the Gospel is revealed the righteousness of God, from faith to faith..."

Our soul is in the process of being saved each time we receive a breakthrough revelation of faith. Spread over a period of our earthly time, our soul transforms in the very image of Christ as we receive our soul's complete spiritual understanding of who we are in Christ. Faith culminates once it reaches the goal of saving the soul.

The status of our soul's character determines what we are capable of manifesting from God. For now, our spiritually immature mind is not capable of handling the full revelation of what our righteousness position in Christ is.

If God ever decided to hit us with the one-time full revelation of our destiny in Christ, it will be so excessively good for our undeveloped soul to grasp.

The ill-equipped character of our soul is not capable of handling such unveiling. A one-time flash of chockfull revelation will inevitably saturate us with a heretic impression. Thus, we will not be able to contain and control it.

Our soul's current spiritual grasp decides what it can now come to terms with God; this is the reason why the revelation towards our soul's salvation is progressive.

One of the dangers of receiving a revelation beyond our capacity to receive is exposure to liability of heresy. If we do not have Christ-centered soul's character that matches the revelation, knowledge will only puff our heads up and subsequently destroy us.

Pride is a malignancy of knowledge in the absence of Christ's character. We saw many examples from the past; ministers who started right but ended up as a cult leader because of their inability to handle the truth. The truth was and still is they are unable to handle the truth!

Yes, a breakthrough is a result of the process of co-laboring with God. Breakthrough is the collaboration of unlimited ability of God and the limited capability of man. We do the doable, and we let God break the impossible. We gain God's supremacy when we break off from our self-dependency.

Breakthrough transpires when by His revelation, we engage ourselves to our perceived prophetic vision. Our breakthrough occurs between our faith's commencement and culmination.

What you are currently is not your finality; greatness always starts from our beginning - Christ. Our soul's completion waits for us at the end. We forge the future when we let God's present grace shapes our past.

Let us keep on breaking to breakthrough.

ENDNOTES

[1] Acts 16:6-10, 16:16-34 The Living Bible
[2] Strong, James. *Strong's Exhaustive Concordance of the Bible*. Updated ed. Peabody, MA: Hendrickson Publishers, 2007.
[3] Read Colossians 2:10 NKJV
[4] Compare it to Matthew 11:12 NKJV
[5] Read 2 Corinthians 10:3-5 NKJV
[6] Meditate on John 8:32 KJV
[7] Read Romans 8:6 NKJV
[8] Read 1 Thessalonians 5:23 NKJV
[9] Read 1 Corinthians 1:30 (Amplified Version of the Bible)
[10] Read 1 Corinthians 3:9 KJV
[11] Read Matthew 11:28-30 KJV
[12] Read 3 John 2 KJV
[13] Read Luke 11:13 NKJV
[14] Read 1 John 3:8 NKJV
[15] Read Matthew 8:27 KJV
[16] Read Romans 5: 14-19 NKJV
[17] See Galatians 1:4 KJV
[18] Read Ephesians 2:10 TPT
[19] Read Romans 12:1-2 NKJV
[20] Read James 4:6-8 NKJV
[21] Read Luke 15:10 The Message Bible
[22] Read Romans 11:36 – 12:1-2 NKJV
[23] See Luke 22:39 The Message Bible
[24] Read 2 Corinthians 3:17-18; 4:1- 5:7
[25] Read John 6:9 NKJV
[26] Meditate on Luke 17:14 NKJV
[27] Read Philippians 4:13 NKJV
[28] Read 1 Timothy 4:7 KJV
[29] Read 1 Timothy 4:8 NKJV
[30] Read Galatians 5:6 NKJV
[31] Read 1 Timothy 4:8 NKJV
[32] *Pleasantville*. Directed by Gary Ross. Warner Bros. Entertainment, 1998. DVD.

[33] Pitts, Barbara Russell. Everything Inventions And Patents Book Turn Your Crazy Ideas into Money-making Machines!. Avon, MA: F W Media, 2010.
[34] Webster, Inc. The Merriam-Webster Dictionary. New ed. Springfield, Mass.: Merriam-Webster, 2005.
[35] Meditate on Romans 8:6 NKJV ('…for to be spiritually minded (soul) is life and peace…")
[36] Read John 9:4 KJV
[37] Read Psalms 115:16 KJV
[38] Sanballat and Tobiah were antagonists to God's plan and His people (Nehemiah 4:1-6 NKJV)
[39] Read Hebrews 11:5-6 NKJV
[40] Read Hebrews 6:1 (BSB)
[41] Read Matthew 5:45 NKJV
[42] Pause and meditate on 3 John 2-4 KJV ("above all things.")
[43] Read Mark 4:9 NASB
[44] Strong, James. Strong's Exhaustive Concordance of the Bible. Updated ed. Peabody, MA: Hendrickson Publishers, 2007.
[45] Read Matthew 10:24-25 NKJV
[46] Read Revelation 12:11 NKJV
[47] Read 1 John 2:12-14 NKJV
[48] Read 3 John 2 KJV
[49] Read Romans 8:19 NKJV
[50] Read Matthew 4:19 NKJV
[51] Read James 4:6-8 NKJV
[52] Read Ephesians 4:22-24 NKJV
[53] Read and Meditate Ephesians 2:10 NKJV
[54] Read 2 Corinthians 1:20 NKJV
[55] Read Hebrews 6:13-15 NKJV
[56] Read John 1:29-34 NKJV (The dove came down on the Lamb – a symbol of meekness.)
[57] Read Psalms 25:10, Jeremiah 33:6, John 1:17, John 4:23-24, Ephesians 5:9
[58] Read Colossians 1:15 NKJV
[59] Read John 14:6 NKJV
[60] Read Isaiah 30:21 NKJV
[61] Read 1 Corinthians 2:13 NKJV
[62] Read Galatians 6:14 KJV
[63] Read Romans 8:6 NKJV

64 Read James 3:7-10 The Message
65 Read Philippians 3:13 NKJV
66 See Luke 6:37-38 NKJV
67 Read John 1:17 NKJV
68 Read Proverbs 10:19 NKJV
69 Read Matthew 26:41
70 Read Galatians 5:23 KJV, Romans 5:5 NKJV
71 Read John 8:37-39 NKJV
72 Read Matthew 16:16-19 NKJV
73 Read Matthew 16:18 Amplified Version
74 Read Ephesians 4:7-16 KJV
75 Read 2 Corinthians 4:3-6 NKJV
76 Read Proverbs 29:18 NKJV
77 Read Matthew 4:4 NKJV
78 Read John 3;3-6 NKJV
79 Read Hebrews 11:1   NASB
80 Read Matthew 26:41 NKJV
81 Read Matthew 9:36 NKJV
82 Read Genesis 1:31 NKJV
83 Read John 14:6 NKJV
84 Read Ephesians 1.3 NKJV
85 Read Acts 10:38 NKJV
86 Jesus unless the Spirit of God enables them
87 Read John 3:34 NKJV
88 Read Acts 5:1-11 NKJV
89 Read Ephesians 2:8-9 NKJV
90 1 Corinthians 12:11 NKJV
91 Read John 13:35 NKJV
92 Read Ephesians 3:16-19 NKJV
93 Read Daniel 11:32 NKJV
94 Read and Meditate on Hebrews 12:1-5 NKJV
95 Read Mark 16:20 NKJV
96 Read Romans 12:21 NKJV
97 Read James 4:6 NKJV
98 Read John 1:14 NKJV
99 Read James 1:17 NKJV
100 Read Titus 2:11-12 NKJV
101 Read 2 Corinthians 3:17-18 NKJV
102 Read Psalms 8 - The Amplified Bible

[103] Read Romans 8:30 NKJV
[104] Read Romans 8:28-29 NKJV
[105] Read 2 Corinthians 5:21 NKJV
[106] Read Romans 8:28-30 NKJV
[107] Read 2 Corinthians 3:17 NKJV
[108] **Read John 5:19 NKJV**
[109] Read Matthew 6:31 KJV
[110] Read Romans 6:13 NKJV
[111] Proverbs 20:5 The Message
[112] Read Proverbs 29:18 NKJV
[113] Read 2 Corinthians 10:5 NKJV
[114] Read Matthew 4:4 TPT
[115] Read Proverbs 4:23 NKJV
[116] Read Psalms 119:11 NKJV
[117] See Revelations 3:10 NKJV
[118] Read Deuteronomy 6:16 KJV
[119] Read 1 Corinthians 15:10 NKJV
[120] Read 2 Peter 1:2-4 NKJV
[121] Read 1 Corinthians 13:9-12 NKJV
[122] Kairos – means a definite appointed time in the plan and purposes of God.
[123] Read Ephesians 5:15-18 NKJV
[124] Read Luke 10:27 NKJV
[125] Back in the 90's, Smokey Mountain is a landfill where two million metric tons of Metro Manila waste is being dumped.
[126] Read Matthew 6:27 NKJV
[127] In Hebrews 10:29; The Holy Spirit is mentioned as the Spirit of Grace.
[128] "G1877 - epanagō - Strong's Greek Lexicon (KJV)." Blue Letter Bible. Accessed 5 Sep, 2016. https://www.blueletterbible.org//lang/lexicon/lexicon.cfm?Strongs=G1877&t=KJV`
[129] Read I John 4:17 NKJV
[130] "G1377 - diōkō - Strong's Greek Lexicon (KJV)." Blue Letter Bible. Accessed 5 Sep, 2016 https://www.blueletterbible.org//lang/lexicon/lexicon.cfm?Strongs=G1377&t=KJV
[131] Read Mark 10:46-52 NKJV
[132] Read Psalms 103:1-5 KJV

www.ingramcontent.com/pod-product-compliance
Lightning Source LLC
Chambersburg PA
CBHW061636040426
42446CB00010B/1451